New Directions for
Higher Education

Martin Kramer and
Judith Block McLaughlin
CO-EDITORS-IN-CHIEF

The Stress of Change: Testing the Resilience of Institutions

Martin Kramer
EDITOR

Number 151 • Fall 2010
Jossey-Bass
San Francisco

THE STRESS OF CHANGE: TESTING THE RESILIENCE OF INSTITUTIONS
Martin Kramer
New Directions for Higher Education, no. 151
Martin Kramer, Judith Block McLaughlin, Co-Editors-in-Chief

Microfilm copies of issues and articles are available in 16mm and 35mm, as well as microfiche in 105mm, through University Microfilms Inc., 300 North Zeeb Road, Ann Arbor, MI 48106-1346.

NEW DIRECTIONS FOR HIGHER EDUCATION (ISSN 0271-0560, electronic ISSN 1536-0741) is part of The Jossey-Bass Higher and Adult Education Series and is published quarterly by Wiley Subscription Services, Inc., A Wiley Company, at Jossey-Bass, 989 Market Street, San Francisco, CA 94103-1741. Periodicals Postage Paid at San Francisco, California, and at additional mailing offices. POSTMASTER: Send address changes to New Directions for Higher Education, Jossey-Bass, 989 Market Street, San Francisco, CA 94103-1741.

New Directions for Higher Education is indexed in Current Index to Journals in Education (ERIC); Higher Education Abstracts.

SUBSCRIPTIONS cost $89 for individuals and $259 for institutions, agencies, and libraries. See ordering information page at end of journal.

EDITORIAL CORRESPONDENCE should be sent to the Co-Editors-in-Chief, Martin Kramer, 2807 Shasta Road, Berkeley, CA 94708-2011 and Judith Block McLaughlin, Harvard GSE, Gutman 435, Cambridge, MA 02138.

Cover photograph © Digital Vision

www.josseybass.com

CONTENTS

EDITOR'S NOTES   1
Martin Kramer

1. Mobilizing for an Outbreak and Its Aftermath   5
Samantha Goldstein
Babson College learns that it can manage and survive a crisis.

2. Conveying the Meaning of the Economic Crisis   15
Luke A. Anderson
Three university presidents publicly frame their responses to the
financial catastrophe.

3. Loss of Accreditation at Historically Black Colleges and   29
Universities
Rhonda E. Baylor
Regaining accreditation is an urgent and immediate task to maintain
an institution's sources of support.

4. Looking for a Way Out   39
Gregory Esposito
Declining state support for public universities can create pressures
for institutions both to resist the decline and adapt to it.

5. Tough Questions Facing Women's Colleges   49
Sara Kratzok
The transition of women's colleges into coeducational institutions
presents fundamental issues and sensitive dynamics.

6. Stress in Senior Faculty Careers   61
Brendan C. Russell
Faculty can find even successful careers more stressful than they
expected.

7. The Future of Shared Governance   71
Matthew A. Crellin
Shared governance between administration and faculty needs to
be viewed as a sanctioned vehicle of collaboration, not a rivalry.

8. The Rose Art Museum Crisis   83
Paul Dillon
A decision to close a famous art museum exposes ambiguities in
governance and leadership.

9. A Contested Institutional Culture   93

Stephanie A. Morin
A new president finds himself at odds with defining traditions of his
institution.

10. Rapid Change and Legitimacy   105

Matthew Waldman
An accumulation of events can force a presidential transition.

INDEX   115

EDITOR'S NOTES

Like other human institutions, colleges and universities can find change highly stressful. Of course, higher education is in some ways all about change. Colleges and universities aim to change students and to advance the frontiers of knowledge. Mission statements state such goals as:

- to develop their students' "creativity, independent thought, and intellectual depth, breadth, and curiosity"
- to help them to "master significant areas of knowledge and skills while developing an appreciation for individual and cultural diversity, a sense of social responsibility and a system of personal and professional ethics"
- "to create knowledge, to open the minds of students to that knowledge, and to enable students to take best advantage of their educational opportunities"

But colleges and universities tend to see the performance of these tasks as requiring a protective environment that allows orderly development, the reflective design of curricula, and the gradual initiation of students into the methodological canons of the disciplines.

To be sure, most colleges and universities have administrative and governance arrangements that can come to terms with change when they must. These can come into play to interpret and modulate change and to allow necessary adjustments through participatory processes. But the capacity of these mechanisms to preserve and protect the institution is not ordinarily all that visible. Gradual and decorous accommodations tend to make the working of these mechanisms largely or even wholly invisible.

It is a premise of this collection of essays that we need to look at highly stressful change to understand, or at least get a feel for, the capacity of governance, administration, and faculty to deal with major issues.

Sometimes the source of change lies in the structure or operation of the governance of the institution itself. Much more often—at least among the institutions represented in this collection—the change results from factors external to the institution. These may be large social movements, economic pressures, or an apparent reduction in demand for the kind of education that has in the past constituted the institution's trademark and mission.

Chapter One of this volume examines the response of one institution to an obviously very stressful event: an outbreak of highly contagious disease. The college needed to mobilize almost every element of its governance and administrative structures to respond, and quickly. All parts of the institution needed to understand the nature of the threat, to minimize the cases of the outbreak, to care appropriately for those infected, and to enable all

NEW DIRECTIONS FOR HIGHER EDUCATION, no. 151, Fall 2010   © Wiley Periodicals, Inc.
Published online in Wiley Online Library (wileyonlinelibrary.com) • DOI: 10.1002/he.395

parts of the institution to return as soon as possible to their normal functions.

More than this, however—and this is characteristic of how institutions of higher education must be able to react to change—the college needed to reassure students, parents, staff, and external constituencies that it was indeed able both to perform normal functions and to conduct itself competently and sensitively in circumstances of great stress. It needed to demonstrate important kinds of resilience for the future.

Chapter Two examines first responses to very different sources of stress: the reaction of institutions with vast investments to the great financial losses resulting from the financial collapse of 2008 and 2009. The institutions in question, Harvard, Princeton, and Stanford, were utterly dependent on returns from these investments, both for their current operations and for plans for the future that had evolved through a long period of very high returns.

These institutions needed to demonstrate an ability to come to terms with their losses and also to reassert their continuing commitment to core purposes. Again, both internal and external constituencies needed to be reassured of the competence of governance and administration. Deciding on the right timing and tone of such reassurance was itself part of the reassurance needed.

Neither epidemic nor financial collapse is targeted specifically at colleges and universities. Chapter Three looks at just such a case of targeting: the threat of a denial of accreditation which could deprive an institution of major financial support and the confidence of students and parents. With neither students or resources, a college or university could die. This chapter examines how several historically minority-serving institutions sought to deal with such a threat and to establish their competence to resume performance of their historical mission.

Some shocks that challenge the viability of colleges and universities come upon them more gradually and are not so much a matter of immediate threat but a growing realization that the future is much less promising than had been supposed. Chapter Four examines how the erosion of projected public funding for public institutions in Massachusetts and Rhode Island resulted in such a challenge. Institutions in this situation need both to make their case for higher levels of support and to assert the continuing viability of their missions even if that support does not soon materialize.

The change that produces stress may not be so much a shock, but a gradual realization that the way the institution frames its mission may no longer closely match the expectations of external constituencies as it did in the past. Chapter Five looks at the situation of women's colleges whose role has necessarily changed as the role of women in society has changed. That situation reopens the most fundamental questions about the missions of these institutions, questions that need answering whether or not any changes of mission, either marginal or fundamental, are in order. Again, both internal and external

NEW DIRECTIONS FOR HIGHER EDUCATION • DOI: 10.1002/he

constituencies have stakes in the outcome, and they often engage in a kind of protracted dialogue before reaching a resolution.

Chapter Six explores the toll of career stress on faculty. In good times for the institution and for individual careers, faculty tend to feel that they are the institution. Not-so-good times bring out the adversarial potential of the relationship.

Faculty obviously has much at stake in all the situations mentioned so far in these notes. They usually also have a role in working out the way the institution will think about and deal with the stress of change. This role itself is, however, subject to change and can be the source of stress. This is the role we have come to call "shared governance." Problems arising from changes in this role are the topic of Chapter Seven. Governing boards, "super boards," and state legislatures increasingly include people who take modern business methods and quantitative accountability as the norm for any sort of enterprise. Academic administrators—presidents, provosts and deans—may consider themselves directed by these competent authorities to embrace these same values and practices. Unless faculty find effective ways to assert their governance role in these changed circumstances, shared governance can become diluted or atrophy.

The capacity of governance and administrative structures to deal effectively with change and somehow to resolve stress can itself be brought into doubt by actions that are viewed as alienating important internal and external constituencies. When this happens, when the institution's ability to work through change while maintaining the institution's mission and purpose is called into question, we see how utterly essential this capacity really is.

Chapters Eight, Nine, and Ten look at cases where such a breakdown has occurred and how large and difficult is the task of restoring a sense of that capacity. These cases are very different from each other:

—In the first, what brought about this kind of breakdown was a governance decision to close, for fiscal reasons, a campus art museum that had become famous and itself part of the institution's reputation for excellence.
—In the second it is the apparent withdrawal of support from symbolic representations of the fundamental traditions of the institution.
—In the third it is the accumulation of apparently routine decisions that come to be seen as illegitimate in the eyes of a larger and larger proportion of people in faculty and administrative positions.

A restoration of legitimacy in such circumstances can then become the crucial first step in coming to terms with change.

This volume is in an important way different from most issues in the *New Directions for Higher Education* series. Ordinarily, an issue editor is invited to ask a set of chapter authors to take up various aspects of a topic. The idea is to plan a group of contributions which, together and conveniently, will enable someone to get up to speed on the topic.

This volume came about in quite the opposite fashion. Rather than selecting an issue editor and theme, with the chapters then commissioned around this topic, these chapters were produced independently without any volume in mind.

The chapters originated as papers produced for a graduate seminar conducted by my co-editor, Judith Block McLaughlin. Believing that the student essays constituted a thoughtful body of research and analysis, we asked all the students in the seminar to submit their papers for my review. From these submissions, I selected those essays that offered important insights into a diverse set of issues related to change and that represented a wide array of higher education institutions.

Perhaps because the authors were students when they conducted their research and not administrators or faculty at the institutions they were examining, they saw many of the situations and circumstances they investigated with fresh eyes. They were not writing trying to put the best light on their own or their institution's actions. They conducted inquiries without a history of past relationships coloring the conversations. Their outsider status may have limited their knowledge in some respects, and individuals at these colleges and universities will have their own interpretations of issues and events that may correspond with or differ from, those presented in the articles. But that, after all, is part of the complexity of change: Change looks vastly different depending on one's placement with regard to it.

NEW DIRECTIONS FOR HIGHER EDUCATION • DOI: 10.1002/he

1

Babson College learns that it can manage and survive a crisis.

Mobilizing for an Outbreak and Its Aftermath

Samantha Goldstein

When the H1N1 virus ascended to national attention in April 2009, colleges and universities in the United States were thrust into the role of managing an unforeseen health crisis. While other institutions were scrambling to coordinate the appropriate crisis response to the H1N1 virus, Babson College was using the lessons it had learned during its recent Norovirus outbreak to coordinate an effective response without panic or paranoia. As novel illnesses continue to emerge in our increasingly globalized society, it is important to explore and understand how institutions respond to unanticipated health crises. Babson's experience with the Norovirus outbreak offers valuable insight into the importance of flexible protocol, decisive decision-making, and coordinated emergency responses that include external constituents as well as internal stakeholders.

Background

Babson College was founded in 1919 by Roger Babson in Wellesley, Massachusetts with the mission of educating the country's next great business leaders. As a master's level institution, Babson's undergraduate and graduate entrepreneurship programs are routinely ranked the top in the nation. Babson is a largely residential campus with 85 percent of the nineteen hundred undergraduate students living in a residential hall. This high residential capacity would also pose a challenge when the Norovirus emerged on campus in early spring of 2009 as campus leaders sought to contain the outbreak while addressing the needs of diverse campus community members.

Norovirus is a highly contagious, surface-surviving virus that causes "acute onset vomiting, watery diarrhea with abdominal cramps, and nausea"

New Directions for Higher Education, no. 151, Fall 2010 © Wiley Periodicals, Inc.
Published online in Wiley Online Library (wileyonlinelibrary.com) • DOI: 10.1002/he.396

(Centers for Disease Control, 2009). Although Norovirus is a relatively common illness that is rarely life threatening and lasts between 24 and 36 hours, it can induce dehydration or other health complications. Norovirus outbreaks have occurred at other college campuses, including Georgetown University (Washington, DC) in October 2008 where over 170 students were sickened and at Hope College (Holland, Michigan) in November 2008, where over 400 fell ill (Kinzie, 2009; "Hope College Estimates 400 Students," 2009). These institutions would later prove to be valuable resources to Babson College as administrators made important internal decisions to combat the virus.

Monday, March 23, 2009 was the first day back from spring break for Babson College. Students, faculty, and staff were looking forward to the end of the year and an uneventful spring. However, business as usual was disrupted by mid-week at the first indications of a serious health issue, as revealed through interviews with Dean Betsy Newman and Dean Dennis Hanno.

The Outbreak: From Concern to Crisis

The first inkling of a campus-wide health issue arose on Wednesday, March 25, 2009. By the end of that day, about thirteen students had visited the on-campus Health Services with symptoms that included vomiting and diarrhea. Director of Health Services, Sharon Yardley, received a phone call from the Athletic Center asking her to send out a campus-wide bulletin stating that two student athletes reported experiencing food poisoning. Before taking action, Yardley contacted Dean of Student Affairs Betsy Newman to inform her about the elevated number of students visiting Health Services for similar symptoms. Yardley doubted that the illnesses were food poisoning and expressed concern that the campus may be contending with the Norovirus. Newman advised Yardley to contact the Wellesley Board of Health to inform them of the suspected illness. In this initial conversation, Newman emphasized that the Board of Health was supportive of the proactive measures that the college was undertaking to contain the illness.

Just two weeks before, Newman had attended a crisis management conference and met a senior-level administrator from Georgetown University, an institution that had dealt with the Norovirus in 2008. One of the earliest challenges he identified during the outbreak was effectively managing the rumors that the illnesses were caused by food poisoning, rather than the Norovirus. Reflecting upon this interaction, Newman identified that addressing the food poisoning rumors immediately would facilitate a more productive and less panicked campus response. That evening, the Dean of the Undergraduate School, Dennis Hanno, joined Newman, Yardley, and other Campus Life representatives for dinner at Babson's main dining hall to dispel any rumors that the Norovirus was food poisoning and to distribute information.

Throughout the day on Friday, March 27, 2009, there was a constant stream of students visiting Health Services. By 4:00 P.M., Health Services had seen twenty-six students complaining of symptoms consistent with the Norovirus in addition to nine students from the previous day. At 6:00 P.M., Health Services closed for the weekend with normal after-hour on-call protocol in place and backup plans for re-opening if necessary. Public Safety began receiving calls and transporting students who were feeling ill to local hospitals. After the fourth student transport at 9:00 P.M., it was clear that Health Services had to reopen to treat students on campus.

By 10:00 P.M., Newman, in consultation with Yardley, coordinated the reopening of Health Services exclusively for students who were experiencing Norovirus symptoms. By 3:00 A.M. on Saturday, March 28, eighty-eight students had reported being ill or had been seen by Health Services. At 3:30 A.M., Newman sent an update to the Crisis Team and the executive members of the President's Cabinet, including President Leonard Schlesinger. The e-mail outlined the actions that had been taken to combat the illness, the need to contact the Massachusetts Department of Public Health to receive support for any institutional decision-making, and the scheduled Crisis Team meeting at 10:00 A.M. on Saturday (B. Newman, personal e-mail communication, Mar. 28, 2009).

A phone call at 9:00 A.M. on Saturday was pivotal in the fight against the Norvirus. Hanno and Newman had been conducting research on Norovirus outbreaks and came across Hope College, a comparable institution that had experienced the virus recently. Newman and Hanno made contact with Richard Frost, dean of students and vice president, and spent an hour discussing Hope's response to the outbreak and any lessons that could be implemented at Babson. During the outbreak, Hope College was temporarily closed by the state due to concerns over the virus's spread. Frost encouraged Newman and Hanno to take proactive steps to voluntarily close Babson to retain control over institutional decision-making. Hanno and Newman took this advice and called President Schlesinger to express their recommendation to close, which entailed cancelling events, reducing the openness of the campus, and supporting students who were already ill in the residential halls. After the 10:00 A.M. Crisis Team meeting, Hanno and Newman contacted the Wellesley Board of Health to "bring them on board" with the decision. The Board of Health expressed concern over Babson's decision to remain open rather than close immediately to handle the outbreak, but Newman and Hanno emphasized their commitment to a non-panicked and deliberate closure that would take time to orchestrate.

Moments after ending the phone conversation with the Wellesley Board of Health regarding Babson's voluntary closure, administrators noticed that Wellesley police cars had parked in front of the main campus entrance, effectively blocking individuals from entering or exiting the campus. A member of the Crisis Team immediately contacted the chair of the Board of Health and expressed concern that the police presence would cause panic and impede the voluntary closure that Babson was attempting to execute. After communicating this to the Board of Health, the Wellesley officers were removed from the gate and replaced by Babson's Public Safety officers.

From 12:00 P.M. to 3:00 P.M., preparations to close campus were made. The Crisis Team was convened with representatives from departments including Public Safety, Health Services, Food Services, Public Relations, Information Technology, Office of Campus Life, and Facilities and tasks were delegated to ensure that the closing would go as smoothly as possible. A Web site was developed that allowed students to self-report the illness and access real-time information about the Babson closing, a document outlining frequently asked questions was drafted, and a media space was erected near campus to deal with the impending national attention. By 3:30 P.M., arrangements to close campus were complete.

At 4:00 P.M., President Schlesinger announced via e-mail that the campus would be closed from Saturday, March 28 at 5:00 P.M. until Wednesday, April 1 at 5:00 A.M., "all non-essential personnel should not report to campus," and students should "remain on campus to limit the spread of the virus" but were free to leave if they chose, an option that many students embraced over the course of the closure (L. A. Schlesinger, personal e-mail correspondence, Mar. 28, 2009). All campus events and classes were cancelled until the campus reopened. The e-mail also explicitly stated that Babson had reached out to the Wellesley Board of Health who, in turn, had also involved the Massachusetts Department of Public Health for guidance. The president's e-mail was followed by a joint press conference at the Wellesley Board of Health building where Babson officials, including Newman, Yardley, and Schlesinger, and Board of Health representatives communicated a unified message regarding the institutional management of the virus. While the campus was closed, Health Services continued treating students and staff members, and resident assistants went door-to-door handing out cleaning materials, dining services coordinated a take-out dining service to limit student congregation, and Facilities sanitized public spaces.

The Consolidation of Crisis Response Power to the Deans

The purposes and roles of Deans at every institution are different, meaning that their involvement in crisis management can vary widely. Prior to the Norovirus outbreak, Newman was designated as the individual responsible for "coordinating, developing, and employing the Babson College Crisis Management Plan" with the purpose of quickly unifying various departments and managing their "separate and significant areas of responsibility" (Babson College, 2009). In planning for crises and outlining the response expectations for the Dean of Students, the Crisis Management Plan is clear that it is not possible to plan for every crisis. Rather, each emergency should be approached in a "temperate manner" using "good judgment and sensitivity."

The written protocol is always available, along with a crisis response matrix, to all authorized administrators via a secured campus-wide intranet site.

For the purposes of managing this urgent health crisis, President Schlesinger authorized Hanno and Newman to engage in decision-making and directly manage the Crisis Team. Hanno and Newman both pointed out that even with this authorization, it is still not entirely clear whether they should have been the ones managing this specific one due to its scale and public health implications. However, Hanno as dean of the Undergraduate School directly oversees such diverse offices as the Registrar, Athletics, Student Affairs, and Finances, meaning that his day-to-day administrative roles stretch beyond academia and into the realm of student life. His wide net of jurisdiction suggests that whether or not he was officially the "official designee" for managing the crisis, he would have a large amount of involvement in coordinating decisive and effective responses on behalf of the students. As dean of Student Affairs, Betsy Newman has direct oversight of Campus Life, Health Services, and Public Safety, and her leadership of these departments enabled her to mobilize them in response to the virus. For Newman and Hanno, their student-centric job descriptions, coupled with their abilities as effective leaders with multidimensional relationships and jurisdiction across campus made them a strong team to help address the crisis.

During post-outbreak debriefing sessions, the deans faced some criticism for decisions that they made internally. Some executive-level administrators were concerned over who was and was not involved in the Saturday morning Crisis Team meeting and whether they should have been involved sooner, although key executive leaders, including the president, had been briefed of the situation beginning on the Wednesday before closure. There was also some disagreement over how the crisis response groups were identified and coordinated. The Crisis Team representatives were not always the most senior-level administrators within each department, but instead those who could be the most effective in taking action. In addition, because the Norovirus is so contagious, individuals on the Crisis Team also fell ill themselves, leading to the necessity of developing extensive contingency plans to account for the influx of leadership.

With the information that was available at the time of the outbreak, as well as the general need to consolidate power to actors who could quickly and decisively implement change, consolidating power to the deans was appropriate and necessary. However, having a formal plan regarding the delegation of leadership roles in the Crisis Team may have alleviated some internal disagreement over who could and should orchestrate each department's response. The coordination of a multitude of departments across campus was pivotal in Babson's ability to holistically brainstorm and implement the necessary measures to decrease the severity of the outbreak. Hanno and Newman's flexibility and willingness to involve external support networks, including colleagues at other institution and government entities, indicates their willingness to collect and reflect upon information from a variety of sources before making a decision.

Relationship with the Wellesley Board of Health

As suggested by the communications issued by the deans and the President's Office, involving the Wellesley Board of Health was an important step in legitimizing the actions taken by the college to combat the illness. Hanno and Newman both indicate that they actively reached out and asked the Board of Health to become involved in the crisis management process. Neither Newman nor Hanno had any previous experience in managing health crises, and the Wellesley Board of Health played an important role in the media management component of the outbreak. As Babson prepared to reopen, the Board of Health supported the decision, with President Schlesinger's office issuing a public health advisory on March 31, 2009, stating, "throughout the past six days we have been consulting on an ongoing basis with the Wellesley Board of Health and the Wellesley Health Department. Both have expressed full support for our decision to reopen at this time and for our planned actions going forward" (Babson College Office of the President, 2009).

When the reopening was announced, Marcia Testa Simmonson, the vice chairman of the Wellesley Board of Health stated, "what we perceive now is a time that the school can be reopened safely" (Zak, 2009). By involving the Wellesley Board of Health in a proactive yet controlled way, Babson was able to use the Board of Health to legitimize the campus's reopening while retaining control of the decision-making process. Newman reflected that the Board of Health was a supportive partner, but that Babson had to rely on its own resources to manage the incident because it was able to handle the outbreak in flexible and customized phases.

Relationship with Other Community Members

Located in a wealthy residential area of Massachusetts, "town-gown" relations between Babson and the surrounding Needham and Wellesley communities are generally positive. Seeking to be a good neighbor, Babson was committed to transparency with the surrounding community. Although the campus hotline was mainly set up to address inquiries about the Norovirus from students and parents, concerned neighbors were welcome to call to receive more information, and a list of neighborhood-related talking points were developed to address any community questions or concerns.

Parents of current students also represented an important constituency that had to be informed of campus events in a timely manner. Newman and Hanno were aware that announcing the closing of the school without the proper preparations in place could result in a parental panic that could create a more difficult environment to contain the virus. In addition to the hotline and Web site, parents were e-mailed updates daily from the President's Office. By creating multiple avenues of communication, such as e-mails, hotlines, and Web sites, through which individuals could get information, Babson was able to effectively and thoroughly communicate necessary information to multiple stakeholders.

One serious challenge facing Babson during the outbreak was its physically close and semi-integrated relationship with the Franklin W. Olin College of Engineering. As a relatively new and very small institution, Olin students, faculty, and staff regularly utilize Babson's facilities. During the outbreak, Olin chose not to close, but instead implemented heightened sanitation protocols, launched an educational campaign on preventing the spread of the virus, and discouraged students from interacting with Babson students or Babson's campus. This tactic appeared to have been effective; only one faculty member and two students exhibited symptoms consistent with the illness (Hatch and Wasserman, 2009). Any institution that has a symbiotic relationship with another should have an individualized crisis response plan in addition to a plan that will ensure its continued functioning during the closure of the partner school.

Reopening Campus

Over the course of the closing, the campus was thoroughly disinfected and cleaned. On Monday, March 30, only five students visited health services, indicating that the outbreak had peaked. At 5:00 A.M. on Wednesday, April 1, 2009, Babson College reopened and all students, faculty, and staff were welcomed back to campus. In one of his last public updates, President Schlesinger reiterated that the decision to close Babson was correct and effective in "stabilizing the situation" and reducing the outbreak's severity. From reopening, the number of cases continued to sharply decline and by Monday, April 6, an evening health advisory from the President's office heralded that Babson was back to its "high octane activity level" (Babson College Office of the President, 2009).

By the conclusion of the Norovirus outbreak, a large swath of the campus community had fallen ill: 359 students, 55 faculty, staff, and on-campus spouses/partners, 4 Sodexo employees, 4 visiting students, 4 admissions visitors, 4 Olin students, 1 alum and 1 visitor had either seen Health Services or self-reported the illness via an online form (Newman, 2009). As these numbers suggest, the virus hit nearly every campus constituent. However, the majority of the campus population remained healthy.

Long-term Changes

Since the Norovirus outbreak, there has been an ongoing assessment and development of emergency response protocol. Clearer protocols that clearly designate roles and responsibilities have been defined and will better equip

NEW DIRECTIONS FOR HIGHER EDUCATION • DOI: 10.1002/he

the college to address time-sensitive emergencies. Although Hanno and Newman were able to take several hours to prepare the campus for closing, Babson is fully aware that this time line may not be appropriate for all incidents. There has also been dialogue regarding who should coordinate emergency response and how consistent messaging regarding crises could and should be developed. When asked how Babson was so successful in managing the Norovirus outbreak, many of those interviewed cited the fact that it is a small, interconnected campus that values the experiences of its student, staff, and faculty. Babson's size may be helpful in many ways in terms of coordinating emergency response, but may also pose challenges in the future if a more devastating or departmentally fragmenting emergency occurs, a possibility which is being planned for in new emergency response protocols.

There have been changes to the day-to-day operations of how Babson functions. Babson has implemented increased sanitation practices that include weekly bathroom cleanings for all upperclassmen suites. Sanitation stations containing hand sanitizer have been erected to facilitate cleanliness as faculty, staff, and students travel across campus. Months after the outbreak, Public Safety, Health Services, the Office of Campus Life, and the President's Cabinet attended a two-day disaster planning summit that formally trained all of these departments on timely and thorough disaster response.

Lessons for Other Institutions

No institution wants to be known for a serious virus outbreak; however, Babson's handling of the situation reveals important lessons for other institutions in how to coordinate large-scale responses to public health emergencies. Administrators and staff members shared similar advice for other institutions, including having clear and consistent emergency protocols already in place, ensuring that all crisis team responders are familiar with each other and the other departments involved, and facilitating centralized locations where clear and consistent communications can take place. In managing external constituents and messaging, Newman and Hanno emphasized that they were committed to reaching out to external resources, being transparent with stakeholders, and facilitating diverse communication opportunities. Above all else, Hanno and Newman emphasized the importance of staying in front of crises and not being afraid to ask for help when it is needed.

Coordinating a response similar to Babson's may be more challenging at a larger school that has to contend with more students, staff, faculty, and external stakeholders in addition to a larger campus to clean and more media attention. Response coordination may also prove challenging at institutions with more commuter students, as identifying or containing the outbreak may be less straightforward than simply closing campus. Other institutions should make sure that there is sufficient protocol in place to facilitate the closing of the college or university for either short-term or long-term situations. Response protocols that are already in place should be sufficiently flexible to facilitate the development of new protocols as necessary. Finally, institutions should ensure that good personal hygiene is practiced across campus and augmented by professional cleanings of public and private space.

Conclusion

Much of Babson College's success in this emergency can be attributed to the strong leadership of Hanno and Newman; nevertheless, credit should also be directed at the staff members who worked on campus while it was closed to ensure that students were safe and well cared for. At reopening, and for the next few days afterwards, President Schlesinger publicly thanked staff and faculty who contributed to the smooth closing and reopening of campus, a gesture that reiterated how important the campus community is in responding to emergencies. As Babson moves forward from the crisis and contends with new emergencies, its handling of the Norovirus sets a strong example for how to manage crises at an institutional level and has given many administrators at the institution confidence in their ability to handle stressful and highly public situations. By understanding how decisions were made and what ramifications emerged at Babson College, other institutions can reflect upon and develop their own systems for responding to large-scale public health crises in a way that addresses the needs of faculty, staff, and students as well as external constituents who may become involved as the process unfolds.

References

Babson College. "Crisis Program Mission." Unpublished document, Babson College, Wellesley, Mass., 2009.

Babson College Office of the President. "Public Health Advisory." Unpublished document, Babson College, Wellesley, Mass., March 31, 2009.

Babson College Office of the President. "Health Advisory." Unpublished document, Babson College, Wellesley, Mass., April 6, 2009.

Centers for Disease Control. "Norovirus: Technical Fact Sheet." Retrieved December 1, 2009, from http://www.cdc.gov/ncidod/dvrd/revb/gastro/norovirus-factsheet.htm

Hatch, K., and Wasserman, A. "Babson and Olin Deal with Novovirus [sic] Outbreak." Retrieved December 1, 2009, from http://www.wickedlocal.com/needham/news/lifestyle/health/x1098980899/Babson-and-Olin-deal-with-novovirus-outbreak

"Hope College Estimates 400 Students, Staff Struck by Norovirus-Like Illness" Grand Rapids Press, Nov. 10, 2008. Retrieved December 1, 2009, from http://www.mlive.com/news/grand-rapids/index.ssf/2008/11/hope_college_estimates_400_stu.html

Kinzie, S. "Norovirus Behind Illnesses Among Georgetown Students." The Washington Post, Oct. 3, 2008, B01. Retrieved December 1, 2009, from http://www.washingtonpost.com/wp-dyn/content/story/2008/10/02/ST2008100202174.html

Newman, B. "Managing a Crisis: Before, During, and After." Paper presented at the National Association of Educational Buyers (NAEB) Conference, Hyannis, Massachusetts.
Zak, E. "Wellesley's Babson College Reopens after Virus Shuts Down School." Retrieved December 1, 2009, from http://www.wickedlocal.com/wellesley/news/x1579108967/Wellesleys-Babson-College-reopens-after-virus-shuts-down-school

SAMANTHA GOLDSTEIN is a graduate assistant in the Office of Campus Life at Babson College in Babson Park, Massachusetts.

NEW DIRECTIONS FOR HIGHER EDUCATION • DOI: 10.1002/he

2

Three university presidents publicly frame their responses to the financial catastrophe.

Conveying the Meaning of the Economic Crisis

Luke A. Anderson

In the late summer of 2008, after the 2007–2008 fiscal year's books had closed, the nation's wealthiest universities were confronted with an unfamiliar sight: single-digit endowment returns. Not since 2003 had Harvard University (Cambridge, Mass.), Princeton University (Princeton, N.J.), or Stanford University (Stanford, Calif.) earned less than a 16 percent annual return on their rapidly expanding investment portfolios (Figure 2.1). But the early months of 2008 had seen unusually turbulent financial markets. The broad S&P 500 Index had lost 13.1 percent during the year, and the Trust Universe Comparison Service, a large group of investing institutions against which many university endowments measure themselves, had a median return of negative 4.4 percent (Kaplan and Mendillo, 2008). Against this bleak backdrop, Harvard, Princeton, and Stanford managed to outpace all indices, achieving positive 8.6, 5.6, and 6.2 percent returns, respectively (Figure 2.1). Their endowments had each grown, although by a more modest margin than in recent years, to all-time highs, led by Harvard's record sum of $36.9 billion. It had been a challenging year in some sectors of the financial markets, but through investment diversification and the expertise of their teams of money managers, all three universities had emerged unscathed.

Things Fall Apart

Any lament over the prior year's tepid investment gains evaporated during the historic week of September 15, 2008, when major Wall Street firms collapsed and the credit markets froze up instantly, depriving businesses of the basic ability to borrow or invest cash for short periods. The broad financial

NEW DIRECTIONS FOR HIGHER EDUCATION, no. 151, Fall 2010 © Wiley Periodicals, Inc.
Published online in Wiley Online Library (wileyonlinelibrary.com) • DOI: 10.1002/he.397

Figure 2.1 Endowment-Related Statistics, 2000–2009

Fiscal Year Ending	2000	2001	2002	2003	2004	2005	2006	2007	2008	2009
A. Investment Returns Accruing to Endowment										
Harvard University	32.2%	−2.7%	−0.5%	12.5%	21.1%	19.2%	16.7%	23.0%	8.6%	−27.3%
Princeton University	35.5%	2.4%	2.2%	8.2%	16.8%	17.0%	19.5%	24.7%	5.6%	−23.5%
Stanford University	39.8%	−7.3%	−2.6%	8.8%	18.0%	19.5%	19.5%	23.4%	6.2%	−25.9%
B. Endowment Value, End of Fiscal Year						($ in millions)				
Harvard University	$19,148	$18,259	$17,518	$19,295	$22,587	$25,853	$29,219	$34,912	$36,927	$26,035
Princeton University	$8,398	$8,359	$8,320	$8,730	$9,928	$11,155	$12,992	$15,734	$16,349	$12,614
Stanford University	$8,886	$8,250	$7,613	$8,614	$9,922	$12,205	$14,085	$17,165	$17,214	$12,619

Sources: Harvard University, 2008a, 2009b; Princeton University, 2008a, 2008b, 2009c; Stanford University, 2008a, 2008e, 2009d; National Association of College and University Business Officers, 2010.

Figure 2.2 Time Line of Public Messaging on the Economic Crisis, October 2008–April 2009

Date	Harvard	Princeton	Stanford	Brief Description of Communication	Length
October 30, 2008			•	President Hennessy & Provost Etchemendy write to faculty and staff.	705 words
November 3, 2008		•		President Tilghman speaks at a faculty meeting.	*
November 10, 2008		•		Provost Eisgruber and CFO Ainslie speak at a community forum.	*
November 11, 2008	•			President Faust writes to the community.	1,006
November 14, 2008			•	President Hennessy writes to the community.	778
December 2, 2008	•			President Faust & EVP Forst write to the community.	1,120
December 2, 2008			•	Provost Etchemendy writes to the community.	907
December 17, 2008		•		President Tilghman writes to alumni in the weekly newsletter.	845
January 8, 2009		•		President Tilghman writes to the community.	2,311
January 22, 2009			•	Provost Etchemendy speaks to the faculty senate.	*
February 18, 2009	•			President Faust writes to the community.	2,034
March 9, 2009			•	Provost Etchemendy writes to the community.	1,019
April 6, 2009		•		President Tilghman writes to the community.	1,291
April 30, 2009			•	President Hennessy speaks at annual Academic Council meeting.	3,290

*No transcript is available; these messages were documented either in presentation slides or in university news articles.

markets were sent into a tailspin. In the ten weeks following the news of Lehman's collapse, the Dow Jones Industrial Average lost 34 percent of its value. As autumn and winter progressed, the crisis deepened. Value was destroyed in all classes of investments, from natural resources and real estate to private equity and emerging markets. As a result, even the most carefully diversified investors, including many of the nation's universities, could not rely on the strength of one investment to counteract losses in another. American colleges and universities collectively lost at least $120 billion in endowment value from July 2008 to April 2009, and more than one-eighth of that total was lost by Harvard, Princeton, and Stanford alone (Moody's Investors Service, 2009; National Association of College and University Business Officers, 2010).

Endowment losses were only part of an unlikely confluence of events that severely challenged the resilient business model of higher education in late 2008. In an industry report issued in April 2009, Moody's Investors Service called it the worst shock to the higher education sector in decades.[1] Universities faced threats not only from the deteriorating financial markets, but from the drops in home values and escalating unemployment that would put increasing pressure on future tuition and fundraising revenues. Perhaps counterintuitively, the wealthiest institutions were among the first to feel the impact of the swift downturn. The probable reasons for this were twofold: The complex investment strategies that had propelled their vast gains in the prior decade proved difficult to liquidate in the midst of the market crisis; and they had grown increasingly dependent on endowment income to support their growing budgets and ambitious plans.

Faced with the sudden onset of a major crisis, what did the leaders of these institutions do in response? This chapter documents the early public reactions of the presidents of Harvard, Princeton, and Stanford, three of the nation's four wealthiest universities,[2] and identifies themes and disparities in the framing of the problem and the evolving remedies presented by each administration over the remainder of the tumultuous 2008–2009 academic year.

Setting the Tone and Assessing the Damage: October 2008–January 2009

An informal review of the news stories on the Web site of a university president would turn up almost entirely positive messaging. In the public sphere, presidents are seen announcing new programs and initiatives, inspiring confidence among alumni, and encouraging a sense of community among their students. When they speak on the record, one could typically imagine them making their statements with a smile. But presidents were forced to step into the spotlight several times in the six months that followed the market collapse with far more somber messages to deliver. In the first months of the crisis, they and their senior leadership teams had imperfect knowledge of a rapidly evolving situation for which there was no script, and changes in both their tones and their plans were inevitable.

The Presidents Speak. For a period of about six weeks after the mid-September collapse, the presidents of Harvard, Stanford, and Princeton remained silent on the matter of how the economic events had affected their institutions. The first of the three to come forward was John Hennessy, a computer scientist who assumed leadership of Stanford in 2000. In a public letter to faculty and staff on October 30, he struck a tone that mixed optimism with realism: "[W]hile we will have to make significant reductions in our expenses, we will not abandon our core university principles as we navigate these financial challenges" (Stanford University, 2008b). He submitted warnings on a number of fronts, from weaker revenue sources to delayed construction and modest salary increases, and projected that Stanford would need to cut its budget by 5 percent in the following year. He reassured his colleagues that Stanford would act "decisively, but not foolishly," and challenged them to adopt a calm and pragmatic mindset. "After a period of rapid growth," he explained, "it can be healthy for an institution to pause and examine its strategic priorities."

Two weeks later on November 14, Hennessy followed his letter to his colleagues with an appeal to the broader Stanford community of students, parents, and alumni. His message, though similar in content, was framed with this very different audience in mind. "Financial Aid Commitments Still Secure" was the title of the first section, and throughout the letter Hennessy emphasized that Stanford would meet its financial commitment to its students and even reconsider the needs of families who were particularly affected by the downturn (Stanford University, 2008c).

Meanwhile, only a few days earlier on November 10, Drew Gilpin Faust, a historian and the president of Harvard since July 2007, issued a long letter addressed to both of these audiences: her colleagues and her students (Harvard University, 2008b). She cited Harvard's resilience in weathering storms through the centuries, but did not downplay the severity of the moment. "[W]e must recognize that Harvard is not invulnerable to the seismic financial shocks in the larger world," she stated. "Our own economic landscape has been significantly altered." Like Hennessy, Faust promoted a shift in traditional patterns of thinking. "We have to think not just about what more we might wish to do," she explained, "but what we might do at a different pace or do without. Tradeoffs and hard choices that can be avoided in times of plenty cannot be averted now." She hinted at pending reviews of personnel levels and campus expansion plans, but closed with a hopeful and convicted tone and a pledge to maintain Harvard's financial aid policies.

Although similar to Hennessy in tone and overall message, Faust's opening salvo differed in one key way. Unlike her counterpart, who had already estimated impacts to Stanford's budget in detail, Faust provided only one number: 30 percent. She referred to a report released a few weeks earlier by

Moody's in which it had projected a staggering 30 percent decline in endowments by the fiscal year's end. Though a credible industry observer had printed it weeks earlier, the number took on new significance when cited by Faust. She was the first among her counterparts to acknowledge explicitly and assign a magnitude to the deep losses that could be expected at her institution and across the sector.

Faust resumed the conversation in a letter dated December 2 and coauthored by her new executive vice president, Edward Forst (Harvard University, 2008c). In another first among her peers, Faust departed from the long-standing practice of revealing investment results only at the year's end. She disclosed that in the four months preceding October 31, Harvard's endowment had lost at least 22 percent. But because of its holdings in private equity and other complex vehicles which had certainly deteriorated but could not easily be valued, the actual toll was likely to be even worse. There were far fewer moments of optimism in her second letter; the chips had fallen and Harvard now faced a fundamentally different reality. This, however, did not appear to be the case at Princeton.

Princeton Strikes a Different Tone. Although her counterparts had begun publicly framing the problem and preparing their constituents for the worst, Shirley Tilghman, a biologist and Princeton's president since 2001, waited much longer to engage with her public directly. On November 11, the day after Faust's first letter and between Hennessy's two statements, Princeton published a news story that described two committee meetings at which Tilghman and her team communicated resoundingly positive and reassuring messages (Stevens, 2008). "Princeton is incredibly financially healthy," chief financial officer Carolyn Ainslie was quoted as saying at a community forum on November 10 while presenting a slideshow on the basics of university finances (Council of the Princeton University Community, 2008). At the same forum, Provost Christopher Eisgruber stated that while no institution can be entirely insulated, "there is no sense in which Princeton is especially exposed to the economic climate in which we are right now."

A week earlier, Tilghman herself had stated at a faculty meeting, according to the report, that her administration had assessed the situation, and while their long-term capital plans might be altered, they "see no reason to implement programs such as hiring freezes or budget cuts" (Stevens, 2008). In Tilghman's first written submission on the subject, a brief and at times lighthearted letter in the *Princeton Alumni Weekly* on December 17, she stated that her institution was "better positioned than most to weather these storms. Princeton has a well-deserved reputation for skillful investment of its endowment and prudent oversight of its resources, and those reputations are serving us well" (Tilghman, 2008).

In the November 11 account and in Tilghman's own words, administrators drew repeated attention to the "prudence" exercised in Princeton's long-range planning. In a long letter from Tilghman to her campus community on

January 8, her first in the format made familiar by her peers, she continued the sentiment: "Princeton planned conservatively during the good years, knowing full well that markets go down as well as up. Though this year's downturn is deeper than what anyone could have imagined, Princeton will be able to protect its key assets" (Princeton University, 2009a).

After the initial wave of communications from late October to early January, each president wrote or spoke on the record to his or her constituents one additional time: Faust in February, and Hennessy and Tilghman in April. Although economic conditions had not changed appreciably in the intervening months, all three presidents' prognoses only got worse.

Deteriorating Outlooks and Escalating Responses: February–April 2009

As the academic year wore on and the financial markets showed no signs of improvement, the three universities worked to quantify the damage and refine their planned management actions for the current and coming fiscal years. In the spring of 2009, the institutions issued increasingly grim guidance on the future of their operating budgets, investment returns, staffing decisions, and capital plans.

Budgets. The deterioration within this six-month interval was most visible at Stanford, which had been most forthcoming in its earliest communications about the scope of the problem and its planned remedies. In Hennessy's October 30 letter, he stated that Stanford would need to cut about 5 percent from its operating budget in each of the next two years, and that its several schools and operating units were asked to prepare reduction scenarios of 3, 5, and 7 percent. By December 2, when Provost John Etchemendy wrote to the community (on the same day that Faust and Forst wrote to Harvard), the targeted cut had grown to 15 percent over two years, and the scenarios had shifted to 5, 7, and 10 percent (Stanford University, 2008d). When Etchemendy presented to the Faculty Senate on January 22, he announced that Stanford now planned to cut 10 percent in the first year and 5 percent in the second, and would return yet again to the academic units to request scenarios for potential cuts of up to the full 15 percent cut in the first year alone (Stanford University, 2009a). Finally, in a March 9 letter, Etchemendy delivered the knockout blow, announcing that the full 15 percent cut would happen across the board and in the very next year (Stanford University, 2009b). By September 1, 2009, Stanford was to shed nearly one of every six dollars it had spent the year before. Hennessy framed it in stark terms in an April 30 address: "Going forward, it is best to think about the process we are going through as a rebasing of our budget, rather than as a series of budget cuts that might be someday restored" (Stanford University, 2009c).

Stanford's slide was perhaps most perceptible, due to its frequent public transmissions, but the budgetary outlooks at Harvard and even at Princeton declined sharply as well. In her formal communications, Faust was loath to reveal any particular targets or directives, but a March 18 memo described in a *Harvard Magazine* story revealed Harvard's intention to cut the size of its endowment distribution, or the dollar payout it provides to fund a part of the university's budget, by 8 percent in each of the following two years ("Endowment Distribution to be Reduced 8 Percent," 2009). It was reported on April 14 that this two-year guidance had since been augmented into cuts of 8 percent and 12 percent ("FAS Dean Details $220-Million Budget Gap," 2009). These reductions were to follow recent annual distribution increases of 15 percent and more (Harvard University, 2008a). At Princeton, early talk of minimal impact gave way in April to a 7 percent budget cut and 8 percent endowment distribution decrease in the next year, with another 8 percent decrease likely the year after (Princeton, 2009b).

Investments. Investment return expectations converged to dismal lows. Tilghman revealed in January that Princeton lost only 11 percent from June to October (the same interval in which Harvard lost 22 percent), and issued guidance of full-year losses of 25 percent (Princeton University, 2009a). But in Tilghman's April 6 remarks, Princeton joined the ranks of its two peers in forecasting losses of 30 percent. Stanford's provost even alluded in March to that figure "trending higher" (Stanford, 2009b).

Staffing. Personnel outlooks also devolved steadily. Stanford's October claim of a "quite modest salary program for the next few years" had, in Hennessy's words on April 30, been reduced to this: "A 15 percent reduction requires deep cuts, and we know it will affect hundreds of dedicated employees, but we saw no alternative." Well before alluding to these impending layoffs, Hennessy and other top officials had accepted voluntary salary cuts of up to 10 percent (Stanford University, 2008d). Harvard was also eyeing layoffs and had frozen the next year's salaries for all non-union employees (Harvard University, 2009a). The prognosis was only slightly better at Princeton: Although layoffs appeared to be imminent, small salary increases were preserved for employees making less than $75,000 (Princeton University, 2009b). "The steady growth in both faculty and staff that we have enjoyed over the last 10 years will end," Tilghman described in April, "and the University will have to contract in size."

Capital Plans. Finally, changes to long-term capital plans were also grim, but varied perhaps most widely. Princeton was proceeding with caution, having slowed down its ten-year, $3.9 billion capital plan and shifted into a mode where campus improvement projects were approved on a case-by-case basis and only when funding was fully in hand (Princeton University, 2009b). Hennessy confirmed in April that $1.3 billion of planned construction at Stanford was canceled or delayed, but the $1.7 billion in projects under way would go on as planned: "Halting ongoing projects in the middle of construction would waste money and be foolish" (Stanford University, 2009c). But Harvard had already taken such a step, when, on February 18, Faust wrote again to her community to announce that a landmark $1.2 billion science complex already under construction would be "slowed" and perhaps "paused" after crews completed the massive structure's underground foundation (Harvard University, 2009a). Though still boasting healthy balance sheets by any standard, no longer could any of the three institutions afford to support the nearly limitless appetite for campus improvement and expansion that each had developed during the recent years of plenty.

Concluding Observations

My primary intention here has been to document the events of these six months objectively, but I will venture to draw a few inferences as I close. A close read of the fourteen letters, articles, and speeches that comprise this sequence of communications yields at least two themes that invite further consideration.

Attention to Financial Aid. Early and often, the presidents of all three institutions emphasized their unchanged, and in some cases increasing, commitment to their undergraduate financial aid programs. Each institution made it abundantly clear that while budgets would be slashed, construction plans frozen, and employees put in jeopardy, not a dollar would be redirected from the aid package of any current or future students. Given their market-leading positions and famously generous aid policies, their collective dismissal of this option may not be surprising, but is worth placing in context.

How bold a statement was it, in particular, to preserve undergraduate aid? The figures cited by the presidents for these programs appeared tiny in comparison to the massive cuts being proposed. In the midst of Stanford's draconian cutbacks, Hennessy highlighted an additional $7 million to be met in the following year's aid budget (Stanford University, 2009a). Tilghman proudly reported a $5 million ramp-up in Princeton's financial aid to current students, in a letter otherwise filled with references to sums in the hundreds of millions (Princeton University, 2009a). These universities may have had a fresh memory of the pressure placed on them in January 2008 by the U.S. Senate Committee on Finance, which had issued a public questionnaire to the nation's wealthiest institutions to explore the link between soaring endowments and student access and affordability[3] (United States Senate Committee on Finance, 2008). The financially disproportionate focus on financial aid in the presidents' messages may best be explained not only by their actual resolve to maintain it, but also by a desire to placate a few of their more vocal constituents—parents, media, and politicians—in the midst of crisis.

Trust in Prudent Planning. The question that I found perhaps most intriguing and most elusive was this: What, if anything, was actually different at Princeton? Shirley Tilghman's tone was undeniably more positive in November and December 2008 than that of her two counterparts. Tilghman and her team made repeated references to prudent fiscal planning, particularly as it related to endowment payout discipline during recent years of rapid growth. Merit aside, these claims gave Princeton's early communications a distinctly different tone than Harvard's or Stanford's. To the audiences of these messages, it was, in effect, the difference between "We were prepared for this" and "We could never have prepared for this." As outlined above, however, Tilghman began in January to join Hennessy and Faust in increasingly grim budgetary outlooks and remedial actions. By the end of the six-month interval, there was only a marginal difference in severity among the three schools' plans, though Princeton did appear to be slightly better off in certain areas. I will offer two quite speculative approaches to this question, and leave the reader otherwise to make his or her own judgment.

It is widely held that the organizational structures of Harvard and Stanford are relatively decentralized. Thus, when Hennessy and Etchemendy wrote, their actions were fashioned as requests for budget-cutting submissions from the semi-autonomous academic units, rather than a prescription for university-wide reductions. Had she been more particular in her public messages, Faust might have used similar language. Princeton, by contrast, has a considerably more centralized structure and, possibly because of this, used no language of requests or scenarios and instead simply talked about what it planned to do. In the end, the cuts at all three institutions were broad and deep, and structure likely had little effect. But perhaps at the outset, Princeton's central authority may have provided it a sense of control of the sources and uses of its funds that was missing at its more decentralized and less optimistic peers.

Also providing early comfort to Princeton may have been its apparent trust in the university's prudent planning during the good years, specifically in terms of moderated growth in endowment spending. But in an environment of sudden 25 percent losses or worse, this was unlikely to play a materially different role than the endowment payout strategies at Harvard and Stanford. There is only so much room to maneuver within the natural bounds of endowment policies, between high payouts that jeopardize future needs and low payouts that invite criticism from Congress and others. Moreover, Princeton in 2008–2009 was considerably more endowment-dependent than its peers, drawing more than 45 percent of its operating budget from its investments versus 35 and 30 percent at Harvard and Stanford, respectively (Princeton University, 2009a; Harvard University, 2008c; Stanford University, 2009d). This dependence would likely induce more angst in the wake of sharp endowment losses, not less. I am left to suspect that an appeal to endowment spending prudence could have credibly been made by any of these three institutions, but that given this downturn of historic proportions, none would have ultimately found in it the protection that they sought.

A Story Still Unfolding. In the whirlwind six-month stretch that began in October 2008 and ended in April 2009, the presidents of Harvard,

Princeton, and Stanford were thrust onto the stage in a gripping drama that was played out in a series of monologues. Although the story line and its twists were similar for all three players, they made distinguishing choices in tone, in priorities, and in the frequency and detail of their messages that were certain to make unique impressions upon their audiences. These choices, and their real-time reception by key constituents, may even have helped to shape the remedies and policies that would begin to lead these vaunted institutions out of one of the most serious crises they had ever faced.

We can only wait and watch as these management actions continue to take effect over time. Even if the financial markets recover more quickly than most expect, these and other institutions will not recover their lost wealth for many years.[4] They must accept this as a new reality with a "rebased" budget in the near term, as described by Hennessy, and a more measured pursuit of their institutional aspirations in the long term. Whatever the pace of return to the financial flexibility once enjoyed by the wealthiest universities, the long months of 2008–2009 will not soon be forgotten, and especially not by the leaders charged with the task of understanding the historic year's challenges well enough to begin to address them.

Notes

1.   According to Moody's, the prior low point in the higher education sector's financial health, now eclipsed by the events of 2008, had occurred in the early 1990s and was largely demographic in nature. A gradual decline in high school graduates in the 1980s, as the baby-boom generation matured beyond college-age, reduced student demand and forced institutions to curtail capital investment in their aging physical facilities. The demographic drought was exacerbated by the weak U.S. economy of the early 1990s (Moody's Investor Service, 2009).
2.   Yale University, the second-wealthiest institution in the United States, was not excluded from this discussion for any particular reason, other than to create a more manageable set of three universities for comparison and analysis.
3.   In early September 2008, just days before the economic crisis unfolded, Senator Charles Grassley, the committee's most prominent member, toned down his threats for potential legislation (e.g., of minimum payout rates), suggesting instead that he would propose a new Internal Revenue Services (IRS) form that would require disclosure about "student populations or costs" (Marks and Strauss, 2008).
4.   It may not be intuitive, but in a basic endowment model that assumes a 30 percent loss in Year 1, a 5 percent annual payout rate, and annual investment returns beginning in Year 2 of 8%, the endowment would not return to its Year 1 beginning balance until Year 26.

References

Council of the Princeton University Community. "Minutes of the Meeting of November 10, 2008." Unpublished document, Princeton University, Princeton, N.J. Retrieved May 8, 2009 from http://www.princeton.edu/~vp/cpuc/Minutes/Minutes%202009/Nov%2008%20Minutes.pdf

"Endowment Distribution to be Reduced 8 Percent; Budget Cuts Loom." *Harvard Magazine*, March 19, 2009. Retrieved April 25, 2009, from http://harvardmagazine.com/breaking-news/endowment-distribution-be-reduced-8-percent-budget-cuts-loom

"FAS Dean Details $220-Million Budget Gap; Working Groups to Address 'Reshaping' Academic Activities." *Harvard Magazine*, April 14, 2009. Retrieved April 25, 2009, from http://harvardmagazine.com/breaking-news/fas-dean-details-220-million-budget-gap

Harvard University. "Harvard University Response to U.S. Senate Committee on Finance" [February 25, 2008 Press Release]. Unpublished document, Harvard University, Cambridge, Mass., 2008a. Retrieved April 17, 2009, from http://www.hno.harvard.edu/press/pressdoc/supplements/baucus_grassley.pdf

Harvard University. "Letter from President Faust about the Global Economic Crisis" [November 10, 2008 Press Release]. Unpublished document, Harvard University, Cambridge, Mass., 2008b. Retrieved April 19, 2009, from http://www.president.harvard.edu/speeches/faust/081110_economy.php

Harvard University. "Financial Update from Drew Faust and Ed Forst" [December 2, 2008 Press Release]. Unpublished document, Harvard University, Cambridge, Mass., 2008c. Retrieved April 19, 2009, from http://www.president.harvard.edu/speeches/faust/081202_economy.php

Harvard University. "Letter to the Harvard Community from President Faust" [February 18, 2009 Press Release]. Unpublished document, Harvard University, Cambridge, Mass., 2009a. Retrieved April 19, 2009, from http://www.president.harvard.edu/speeches/faust/090218_overview.php

Harvard University. "Harvard University Financial Report: Fiscal Year 2009." Unpublished document, Harvard University, Cambridge, Mass., 2009b. Retrieved March 6, 2010, from http://vpf-web.harvard.edu/annualfinancial/

Kaplan, R. S., and Mendillo, J. L. "John Harvard Letter." Unpublished document, Harvard University, Cambridge, Mass., 2008. Retrieved April 13, 2009, from http://hmc.harvard.edu

Marks, C. M., and Strauss, N. C. "Senator Grassley Tones Down Threats on Endowment Spending." *The Harvard Crimson*, September 9, 2008, p. 1. Retrieved April 17, 2009, from http://www.thecrimson.com/article.aspx?ref=523990

Moody's Investor Service. "U.S. Colleges and Universities Rating Roadmap: Focus on Special Risks During Recession & Credit Crisis." New York: Moody's Investor Service, 2009. Retrieved May 1, 2009, from Moody's Investor Service, http://www.moodys.com

National Association of College and University Business Officers. "2009 Endowment Study." Washington, D.C.: National Association of College and University Business Officers, 2010. Retrieved March 15, 2010, from http://www.nacubo.org/Documents/research/2009_NCSE_Public_Tables_Endowment_Market_Values.pdf

Princeton University. "Response to Your Letter of January 25" [February 22, 2008 Press Release]. Unpublished document, Princeton University, Princeton, N.J., 2008a. Retrieved April 20, 2009, from http://www.princeton.edu/main/news/archive/S20/40/47O42/Senate-letter.pdf

Princeton University. "Princeton University Report on Investments, 2007–08." Unpublished document, Princeton University, Princeton, N.J., 2008b. Retrieved March 6, 2010, from http://web.princeton.edu/sites/TreasurersOffice/Gateway/Files/ReportOnInvestments2007–08.pdf

Princeton University. "Tilghman Letter on Princeton's Response to the Economic Downturn" [January 8, 2009 Press Release]. Unpublished document, Princeton University, Princeton, N.J., 2009a. Retrieved May 8, 2009, from http://www.princeton.edu/main/news/archive/S23/13/63G01/

Princeton University. "Tilghman Letter Updating the University Community on Princeton's Response to the Economic Downturn" [April 6, 2009 Press Release]. Unpublished document, Princeton University, Princeton, N.J., 2009b. Retrieved May 8, 2009, from http://www.princeton.edu/main/news/archive/S23/90/19E72/

Princeton University. "Report of the Treasurer, 2008–2009." Unpublished document, Princeton University, Princeton, N.J., 2009c. Retrieved March 6, 2010, from http://web.princeton.edu/sites/TreasurersOffice/Treasurer/Files/Public/Reports/2008–2009.pdf

Stanford University. "Stanford University Response to U.S. Senate Committee on Finance" [February 22, 2008 Press Release]. Unpublished document, Stanford University, Stanford, Calif., 2008a. Retrieved April 17, 2009, from http://ucomm.stanford.edu/ news/senate_response.html

Stanford University. "Letter from President Hennessy & Provost Etchemendy to All Faculty and Staff" [October 30, 2008 Press Release]. Unpublished document, Stanford University, Stanford, Calif., 2008b. Retrieved April 17, 2009, from http://budget.stanford.edu/113008_budget.html

Stanford University. "Letter from President Hennessy to Alumni, Parents, and Friends of Stanford" [November 14, 2008 Press Release]. Unpublished document, Stanford University, Stanford, Calif., 2008c. Retrieved April 17, 2009, from http://parents.stanford.edu/newsletter/1108letter.html

Stanford University. "Update from Provost Etchemendy to Stanford Community" [December 2, 2008 Press Release]. Unpublished document, Stanford University, Stanford, Calif., 2008d. Retrieved April 17, 2009, from http://budget.stanford.edu/120208_budget.html

Stanford University. "Leading in Times of Challenge: Stanford University Annual Report 2008." Unpublished document, Stanford University, Stanford, Calif., 2008e. Retrieved April 24, 2009, from http://bondholder-information.stanford.edu/pdf/AR_Financial Review_2008.pdf

Stanford University. "Provost Budget Update to Faculty Senate" [January 22, 2009 Press Release]. Unpublished document, Stanford University, Stanford, Calif., 2009a. Retrieved April 18, 2009, from http://budget.stanford.edu/2010_budget_update_facsen.pdf

Stanford University. "Provost Budget Update to Stanford Community" [March 9, 2009 Press Release]. Unpublished document, Stanford University, Stanford, Calif., 2009b. Retrieved April 18, 2009, from http://budget.stanford.edu/030909_budget.html

Stanford University. "President Hennessy Addresses the State of the University and the Economy" [April 30, 2009 Press Release]. Unpublished document, Stanford University, Stanford, Calif., 2009c. Retrieved May 8, 2009, from http://news.stanford.edu/news/2009/may6/hennessy-speech-academic-council-050609.html

Stanford University. "2009 Financial Review." Unpublished document, Stanford University, Stanford, Calif., 2009d. Retrieved March 6, 2010, from http://bondholder-information.stanford.edu/pdf/AR_FinancialReview_2009_Final.pdf

Stevens, R. "Prudent Planning Helps University Deal with Volatile Economic Conditions." News at Princeton, November 11, 2008. Retrieved April 17, 2009, from http://www.princeton.edu/main/news/archive/S22/64/34E22/index.xml

Tilghman, S. M. "Days Like This." Princeton Alumni Weekly, Dec. 17, 2008. Retrieved May 8, 2009, from http://www.princeton.edu/president/pages/20081217/index.xml

United States Senate Committee on Finance. "Baucus, Grassley Write to 136 Colleges, Seek Details of Endowment Pay-outs, Student Aid" [January 24, 2008 Press Release]. Retrieved April 3, 2009, from http://finance.senate.gov/press/Gpress/2008/ prg012408f.pdf

LUKE A. ANDERSON *is a student at the Harvard Graduate School of Education.*

3

Regaining accreditation is an urgent and immediate task to maintain an institution's sources of support.

Loss of Accreditation at Historically Black Colleges and Universities

Rhonda E. Baylor

For nearly two centuries, historically Black colleges and universities (HBCUs) have provided educational opportunities to millions of students who were disenfranchised from traditional higher education institutions. HBCUs have provided African Americans and international students of color with a sense of self-worth and accomplishment. However, during the last couple of decades, some of these institutions have faced financial and institutional problems. In fact, a number of HBCUs have lost accreditation.

Some higher education professionals argue that HBCUs are no longer needed in American education. I disagree. HBCUs provide an opportunity for students of color to examine their culture and to understand that they can be academically successful. Furthermore, America has not moved to a place of total racial inclusion that renders HBCUs unnecessary. Culture should be celebrated and used to enhance our academic, professional, and personal lives. This chapter provides an examination of accreditation problems at HBCUs. Specifically, I examine the situation at Morris Brown College (Atlanta, Ga.), Barber-Scotia College (Concord, N.C.), and Paul Quinn College (Dallas, Tex.), giving more attention to Morris Brown because of the complexity of its situation. Next, I provide my own analysis as to whether these three schools should close or continue to operate. I also provide specific recommendations for each of the institutions. Finally, I provide four recommendations for HBCUs currently in immediate danger of losing their accreditation.

Morris Brown College

Morris Brown was founded by former slaves in 1881 to educate African American students who were left out of "traditional" American colleges and

NEW DIRECTIONS FOR HIGHER EDUCATION, no. 151, Fall 2010 © Wiley Periodicals, Inc.
Published online in Wiley Online Library (wileyonlinelibrary.com) • DOI: 10.1002/he.398

universities (Gasman, 2009). In 2003, the Southern Association of Colleges and Schools (SACS) revoked Morris Brown College's accreditation, citing the following reasons for deaccreditation: mounting debt, institutional effectiveness, poor record keeping, and difficulties with processing financial aid ("Former Morris Brown College President," 2004). A few months later, the school appealed the decision; however, the appeal was overturned and most of the 1,500 enrolled students transferred to other universities.

It was during Dr. Dolores Cross' tenure as college president from 1998 to 2002 that Morris Brown's troubles escalated. In 2004, Dr. Cross was indicted on thirty-four counts of committing financial aid fraud. Allegedly, the former president embezzled $5 million from the U.S. Department of Education by obtaining student loans using the names of former students and students who never attended the college ("Former Morris Brown College President," 2004). Along with Dr. Cross, the financial aid director, Parvesh Singh, was also indicted. After Singh obtained $4 million worth of ineligible loans and was cut off by loan officials, he coaxed his staff into obtaining nearly $1 million more in loans ("Former Morris Brown College President," 2004). The problem was discovered as students who never attended Morris Brown College had trouble obtaining financial aid at other schools because they were told that they had defaulted student loans. Cross's indictment also alleged that during her first year as president she increased school spending by $8 million. Allegedly, she used these funds to hire extra staffers, speechwriters, and housekeepers for her own use ("Former Morris Brown College President," 2004). In May 2006, Dr. Cross pleaded guilty to embezzling funds and was sentenced to five years probation ("Morris Brown President Sentenced," 2007). Her sentence was based on the fact that Dr. Cross did not benefit personally from the crime. Instead, she used the embezzled funds to pay some of the college's operating costs ("Morris Brown President Sentenced," 2007). Parvesh Singh was also sentenced to five years probation.

Some Morris Brown supporters have been very critical of the media's treatment of the situation. Former President Cross's provost and vice president of academic affairs, Dr. Grant Venerable, referred to the indictment as a "modern-day lynching" ("Former Morris Brown College President," 2004). Dr. Venerable stated that Dr. Cross's indictment was partly due to racism and racists who did not want to see a Black woman lead a university. Dr. Venerable also stated that the evidence for the indictment was questionable. In addition, Dr. Venerable argued that if this situation could happen to Morris Brown, it could happen to any of the HBCUs. Lastly, he called for more solidarity among the nations HBCUs ("Former Morris Brown College President," 2004).

Even though student enrollment decreased significantly after these events, Morris Brown continued to operate. In December 2008, city officials cut off the water at the college because of an unpaid $380,000 water bill. The large bill had been accumulating since 2004. By this time, the college was $32 million in debt (Sander, 2008). The college was also short on funds for operating expenses such as faculty and staff salaries (Sander, 2008). To exacerbate the college's financial situation, after the financial scandal, the school's endowment decreased to zero. In 2004, the school only received $203,189 from alumni giving (Seymour Jr., 2006).

Morris Brown College has tried to revive itself in several ways. One year after it lost its accreditation, nationally syndicated radio personality Tom Joyner donated $1 million to the college. Later, Joyner offered to purchase the college because he believed that his foundation could revitalize it. Morris Brown administrators seriously considered this possibility; however, they decided that this would not be the most effective way to restore the university.

Many have reluctantly raised the question about whether Morris Brown and other struggling HBCUs should close their doors to students permanently. "Do we really need the weaker HBCUs?" they ask (Gasman, 2009). One perspective is that these "weaker" colleges hurt the image of all HBCUs. Some people have suggested that the struggling Morris Brown merge with Clark-Atlanta University; others have recommended that Morris Brown become a junior college of the Atlanta University Center. An affiliation with Georgia State University was another consideration (Gasman, 2009).

By the fall of 2008, Morris Brown offered only forty-eight courses to sixty students. Morris Brown is now addressing several lawsuits filed by current and former students. One of the lawsuits was filed by a group of students who did not receive all of their credits because of the financial aid scandal. Another lawsuit, filed by a group of former students against the school's Board of Trustees, calls for trustees to relinquish their positions (Seymour Jr., 2006). There is also a lawsuit to foreclose on three of the school's buildings. In the fall of 2009, Morris Brown increased its student body to 240 students. The current president of Morris Brown College, Stanley J. Pritchett Sr., has developed some aggressive initiatives to stabilize the college.

Barber-Scotia College

Founded in 1867, Barber-Scotia College is one of America's oldest HBCUs. Barber-Scotia's troubles started during the fall of 1994 when the college was placed on probation by its accreditation agency. In 1995, the Southern Association of Colleges and Schools gave Barber-Scotia College two years to stabilize, and the school's administrators did take some initiative to address these concerns. However, Barber-Scotia College had numerous problems that led to the revocation of its accreditation. Professors complained to the state that they were not being paid on time. The school owed $75,000 for unpaid utility services (Kelderman, 2009). Barber-Scotia also failed to collect tuition and other fees from students, creating cash flow problems (Powell, 2004).

Between 1997 and 2003, Barber-Scotia's enrollment grew to a record level of 750, and the institution received a $7 million loan from the U.S.

Department of Education. However, this was still not enough; in 2004, the school lost its accreditation. At this point, the Board of Trustees gave the president, Sammie Potts, the choice of resigning or being terminated (Kelderman, 2009). That year the Southern Association of Colleges and Schools discovered that Barber-Scotia awarded thirty diplomas to students who did not complete the necessary requirements. In January 2005, Barber-Scotia had zero students enrolled and temporarily shut down.

Currently, the school is aggressively trying to raise $10 million by June 30, 2011 (Groover, 2009). The school has $11 million worth of debt and can neither afford to maintain the buildings on campus nor demolish them (Kelderman, 2009). Renting out facilities such as its Olympic-sized pool is a possible source of income; however, the school cannot even afford to maintain it. Currently, the school operates with twenty full-time employees and twelve students with less than $200,000 in cash (Kelderman, 2009).

Paul Quinn College

Paul Quinn College's accreditation was revoked by the Southern Association of Colleges and Schools on June 26, 2009 because the school lacked adequate financial resources and was not academically effective (Appleton, 2009). Students complained of unsanitary, hazardous conditions on the school's campus such as not having hot water in dormitories. A few months later, the university received an injunction that required the Southern Association of Colleges and Schools to reinstate, temporarily, the school's accreditation. Paul Quinn serves approximately 750 students and is the only historically Black college in Texas. Because Paul Quinn is associated with the African-Methodist Church, preachers have been the primary leaders of the college (Appleton, 2009). Unfortunately, unlike Morris Brown College, Paul Quinn has received little assistance from the external community. Alumni's giving is also alarmingly low (Appleton, 2009).

Trouble at Other Historically Black Colleges and Universities

Along with Morris Brown College, Barber-Scotia College, and Paul Quinn College, other HBCUs are in danger of losing their accreditation. Savannah State University and Albany State University are struggling to remain open. Georgia Senator Seth Harp proposed that the two historically Black universities merge with local, predominantly White universities to reduce costs. Heavy opposition from Black educators, politicians, and alumni has been the response to this proposal (Herrmann, 2009). The Southern Association of Colleges and Schools has also issued a "warning" status to two additional HBCUs: Tougaloo College and Florida Memorial University (Jaschik, 2009). Grambling State University, Texas College, Wilberforce University, Fisk

University and Central State University represent other HBCUs that are also currently facing serious financial problems (Hawkins, 2004).

Historically Black Colleges and Universities—Relevant to Higher Education

Some higher education professionals have asked whether HBCUs have become obsolete, arguing that institutions of higher education are now fully integrated. My contention is that racism and segregation have not been sufficiently eradicated in America; therefore, we cannot conclude that HBCUs are no longer needed. HBCUs provide an excellent foundation for millions of African American students throughout the country. I attended one, and I can speak to the profound effect that matriculating at a Black college had on my academic career, as well as on my goals and ambitions. HBCUs provide an opportunity for minority students to see people in higher education who look like them. Self-esteem and confidence can affect learning; attending an HBCU provides Black students with a sense of pride and the understanding that they can be successful. Furthermore, HBCUs provide a significant amount of intellectual human capital to society. According to a 2007 report, historically Black colleges consist of 3 percent of the nation's colleges and universities yet they generate 23 percent of African American college graduates (Schexnider, 2008). In addition, "among Blacks, 40 percent of all congressmen, 12.5 percent of CEOs, 50 percent of professors at non-HBCUs, 50 percent of lawyers and 80 percent of judges are HBCU graduates" (Fryer and Greenstone, 2007, p. 4). According to the American Medical Association, Xavier University produces more medical school students than any other university, Black or White (Schexnider, 2008).

Historically Black colleges and universities provide a comfortable, familiar atmosphere to many Black students who have grown up in urban areas and have had minimum exposure to other cultures. Some may argue that it is best if these students do not attend HBCUs so that they may gain exposure to other ethnic groups. However, this "exposure to other ethnic groups" is not often facilitated properly because university administrators do not make it a priority. This "exposure" has the ability to isolate Black students, causing them to become disengaged from the learning process. It is at this juncture that exposure can turn into a dehumanizing and counterproductive situation. Without HBCUs, far fewer Black students, including international students of color, would have access to post-secondary education.

Should Morris Brown College Close?

Should the HBCUs that have lost accreditation close? This question must be answered based on the circumstances of each individual college. In the case of Morris Brown, I suggest that the college merge with Clark Atlanta University and the Atlanta City University Center as a two-year college that provides clear transition pathways to neighboring Clark Atlanta University, Spelman College, and Morehouse College. Morris Brown must acquire accreditation. To operate without accreditation provides students with a significant barrier to employment. Higher education institutions have a mission to serve students; however, once they lose their ability to do so, they become counterproductive to society.

The fraud scheme involving the former president was a factor in the school losing its accreditation. However, we must recognize that the school was in trouble before Dr. Cross began to allegedly embezzle funds. Although her intentions may have been to help the college, her actions were erroneous and illegal. Dr. Cross had little consideration for the financial repercussions experienced by the students whose names she used to obtain the fraudulent loans. Tom Joyner's offer to purchase the college was generous but probably not in the college's best interest. Morris Brown cannot be saved by a single person. To remain open, it will take a team of dedicated, internal individuals and external supporters. Morris Brown needs to seek leadership and guidance from Spelman and Morehouse College, two of the strongest HBCUs.

Some argue that the college should close completely because of its overwhelming debt load and mismanagement of funds, assuming that it would be nearly impossible for it to recuperate and operate effectively. Some supporters of the college want it to remain open without merging with any other institution. These advocates note that Morris Brown has received a great deal of help from external entities and assert that, with time, Morris Brown will gain its accreditation and operate effectively. I can understand their optimism and recognize that it is difficult to know when to close an institution that has been a pivotal part of a community.

Should Barber-Scotia College and Paul Quinn College Close?

Barber-Scotia College should close and consider selling its property. Sometimes colleges and universities try to distinguish themselves from other businesses by ignoring market conditions and signals. If a business can no longer sustain itself, it closes, reorganizes, or files for bankruptcy. Barber-Scotia operates with twelve students, and I believe that the university is depriving those students of the actual collegiate experience. College students need multiple interactions with many professors and students to gain a spectrum of perspectives.

Prior to losing accreditation, approximately 90 percent of the university's students received financial aid (Kelderman, 2009). Therefore, the school has decreased access to the population that it primarily served because those students cannot receive financial aid to attend the institution. The mission of colleges, especially HBCUs, is to increase college access. Operating a school that cannot provide the financial aid its students depend on is a contradiction of the college's mission.

NEW DIRECTIONS FOR HIGHER EDUCATION • DOI: 10.1002/he

Paul Quinn should try to remain open because it still has its accreditation even though it is temporary. The fact that a judge granted the reinstatement leads me to believe that the school can operate effectively if it makes a few changes. Its accreditation was initially revoked because it failed to meet three standards; I believe that those standards can be met if a culture of strict accountability is implemented. Paul Quinn now has new leadership. Michael Sorrell took over the helm of the college, moving to the presidency from a distinguished career in business and law. I am hopeful that this new leadership will address the serious issues that threaten the college's accreditation.

Possible Corrective Actions

In this final section, I identify various actions that, based on my research, seem promising approaches to solving the crisis facing HBCUs. First, the financial records of those universities who have not yet lost accreditation but are in serious financial trouble should be examined. This would include Savannah State University, Albany State University, Tougaloo College, Florida Memorial University, Grambling State University, Texas College, Wilberforce University, Fisk University and Central State University. These institutions should develop a team consisting of the president, chief financial officer, financial aid director and admissions representatives from each of the schools. No outside consulting agencies except for the Southern Association of Colleges and Schools and other necessary accreditation agencies should be solicited because of the excessive costs. Accountants should immediately help these universities understand their trouble areas. This examination should be conducted at the listed nine universities simultaneously because of the situation's urgency.

A reoccurring problem is lack of funds; hence, these universities must immediately cut costs. Businesses often reduce costs by laying off employees; however, this is not the first option to pursue here. Immediate furloughs, requiring employees to take days off from work without pay, should be implemented based on salary for every employee of the university, including the president and high-level administrators. During this period of salary reductions, these universities must ensure that all utility bills are current and that other more substantial debts are paid on time and as agreed by the creditor and the university. Hiring should be temporality frozen until each college meets some of its financial goals.

The nine troubled universities must generate cash flow immediately. In times of financial hardship, price increases are difficult to accept. However, as the economy grows, the costs of goods and services rise. Just as students have learned that they must pay more for their food, clothing, and housing, they must pay more for their education. HBCUs must remain competitive, and competition involves better services, which come with a more expensive price tag. Each of the troubled universities should implement a 5 percent tuition increase to generate additional, needed funds and provide a greater cash flow that can be used to pay debt and to cover operational costs.

Each university needs to increase its endowment campaign for funds from alumni, corporations, and foundations. This source of potential revenue will add to the schools' operating fund. The presidents of the nine universities should collaborate with presidents from universities with successful fundraising operations to learn strategies. The universities must set a benchmark for increasing the endowment. All goals should be specific, measurable, and realistic with time constraints.

Along with finances, lack of adherence to academic standards is another reason that HBCUs are losing accreditation. The nine universities must seek to develop a thorough understanding of the requirements and the necessary conditions for accreditation. The Southern Association of Colleges and Schools and other accrediting bodies provide very specific information about what is required for accreditation. The president and senior-level administrators from every department should meet to develop a complete understanding of accreditation requirements. During this meeting, each senior-level administrator must develop a plan for what his or her department will do to keep accreditation.

Next, the nine troubled universities should collaborate with the Southern Association of Colleges and Schools and the other necessary accrediting bodies to ensure that academic standards are being met. Universities that are under the same accrediting bodies should hold joint meetings with accrediting representatives to discuss specific issues that the schools face. Administrators should implement an audit system that ensures that the universities are held accountable for accreditation standards. Along with these joint meetings, the universities must request that members from the accrediting bodies conduct onsite visits prior to the accreditation review period. Representatives from the various accrediting bodies should visit each campus monthly until they are no longer in danger of losing accreditation.

The future of HBCUs is threatened. Effective leadership is important if HBCUs are going to survive. Xavier President Dr. Norman Francis offers this observation: "Make sure that leaders in industry, business, state and local officials know what you can do, and what you can contribute. . . . If it is thought that you have no contributions to make, then you must be a liability" (Hawkins, 2004). I recommend that presidents and provosts at HBCUs have some type of business background combined with an academic background. Most of the HBCUs that are in crisis are in financial crisis because of mismanagement of funds. Professional managers from the corporate sector are familiar with minimizing costs and maximizing revenue. This model needs to be implemented at these colleges.

Presidents and other high-level administrators must view the operation of the university as similar to the operation of a business. Leadership at this level must focus on managing money. The president's office and the university's business office should work closely together to ensure that operating expenses are being met and that the university is fiscally strong. Accountability is key, and it will force institutions to act more responsibly with their resources. Senior-level administrators with corporate experience should be sought for some positions to enhance accountability standards. The board of trustees and the president of each university should be responsible for ensuring that accreditation standards are met.

Conclusion

Over the past few decades, accreditation at many of HBCUs has been threatened by growing financial problems, decreased scholarship, and misappropriations by leadership. With questions about the necessity of Black colleges and universities, the accreditation process forces higher education institutions to reexamine their missions and their operational philosophy.

Some critics argue that HBCUs should close because there is no need for them. My contention is that these institutions have proven to be places of opportunity for Black students and international students of color. If it were not for these schools, many minorities would not enter or graduate from college. HBCUs in danger of losing their accreditation should explore the following recommendations: examine financial records and cut costs; raise tuition by 5 percent and increase endowment; collaborate with accrediting agencies and establish monthly audits prior to the reaccreditation process and enhance leadership by recruiting leaders with corporate experience. Although the number of HBCUs in danger of losing accreditation represents only a small percentage of HBCUs, we must act immediately and intentionally to address the problems that these institutions are facing. Higher education leaders need to be held more accountable for their actions and inactions for survival of America's historically Black colleges and universities.

References

Appleton, R. "Paul Quinn College Sues Association over Accreditation. " *Dallas News*, Aug. 26, 2009. Retrieved December 5, 2009, from http://www.dallasnews.com/shared content/dws/news/localnews/stories/DN-paulquinn_26met.ART .State.Edition2.4c0cd87.html

"Former Morris Brown College President, Financial Aid Director Indicted for Fraud." *Diverse: Issues in Higher Education*, December 30, 2004. Retrieved November 29, 2009, from http://diverseeducation.com/article/4215/1.php

Fryer, R., and Greenstone, M. "The Causes and Consequences of Attending Historically Black Colleges and Universities." Cambridge, Mass.: National Bureau of Economic Research, April 2007.

Gasman, M. "Much to Do About Morris Brown College." *Diverse: Issues in Higher Education*, January 6, 2009. Retrieved November 28, 2009, from http://diverseeducation.word press.com/2009/01/06/much-to-do-about-morris-brown-college/

Hawkins, D. "Doing More with Less." *Diverse: Issues in Higher Education*, June 17, 2004, 21(9). Retrieved November 21, 2009, from http://diverseeducation.com/article/ 3759/doing-more-with-less.html

Herrmann, M. "Morris Brown Determined to Survive." *University Business*, February 1 2009, 12(2). Retrieved November 20, 2009, from http://www.thefreelibrary.com/Morris+Brown+determined+to+survive.-a0194101948

Groover, Jessica. "Barber-Scotia College Announces $10 million Comeback". *Independent Tribune*. May 2, 2009. Retrieved December 2, 2009, from http://www2.independenttribune.com/content/2009/may/02/barber-scotia-college-announces-10-million-comebac/

Jaschik, S. "Paul Quinn Loses Accreditation." *Inside Higher Ed*, June 26, 2009. http://www.insidehighered.com/news/2009/06/26/paulquinn

Kelderman, E. "Troubled Barber-Scotia College Seeks Revival." *Chronicle of Higher Education*, October 19, 2009, 56(9).

"Morris Brown President Sentenced to Five Years Probation." *Diverse: Black Issues in Higher Education*, January 25, 2007, 23(25).

Powell, T. "In Not So Good Company." *Black Issues in Higher Education*, August 26, 2004, 21(14). Retrieved December 1, 2009, from http://diverseeducation.com/article/3933/1.php

Sander, L. "As Debts Mount, Morris Brown College Will Not Reopen Next Semester." *The Chronicle of Higher Education*, December 22, 2008. Retrieved December 1, 2009, from http://chronicle.com/article/As-Debts-Mount-Morris-Brown/42158/

Schexnider, A. "Perspectives: The Future of Public HBCUs Depends on Exceptional Leadership." *Diverse: Issues in Higher Education*, February 11, 2008. Retrieved December 1, 2009, from http://diverseeducation.com/artman/publish/article_10631.shtml

Seymour Jr., A. "Morris Brown Hanging on in Wake of Scandal." *Diverse: Issues in Higher Education*, July 13, 2006, 23(11) Retrieved December 1, 2009, from http://diverseeducation.com/article/6108/1.php

RHONDA E. BAYLOR, *Ed.M MBA, is a graduate student at Harvard University.*

NEW DIRECTIONS FOR HIGHER EDUCATION • DOI: 10.1002/he

4

Declining state support for public universities can create pressures for institutions both to resist the decline and adapt to it.

Looking for a Way Out

Gregory Esposito

Declining state support for higher education is not unique to Southern New England nor is it a recent phenomenon. Public universities in the United States relied on state and local funding for about half of their revenue in 1980–1981. By 1999–2000 that proportion had dropped to about one-third (Courturier and Cunningham, 2006). With the recession decimating state coffers, the general decline has hit a cliff in many states. State budgets for 2009–2010 show that only 12 states increased appropriations to public higher education since 2007–2008 (Fain, 2009). State support is declining even more rapidly at public higher education institutions in Rhode Island and Massachusetts. When adjusted for cost-of-living and enrollment mix, only New Jersey and Michigan cut state funding per full-time equivalent student by a larger percentage than Rhode Island (19.1 percent) and Massachusetts (14 percent) from 2003 to 2008 (State Higher Education Finance Report, 2009). Because declining state support is such a widespread, long-standing, and seemingly intractable issue, it is important to examine the recent history and results of low public support for higher education and what future cuts could mean for the two states.

Rhode Island

In Rhode Island, tuition and fees for the three public institutions of higher education have increased 64, 75, and 72 percent, respectively, over the past eight years, and state support for these institutions has fallen by more than $30 million in the past three years (Jordan, 2009b). The state ranked forty-seventh in state educational appropriations to public higher education per full-time equivalent student in 2008, with the $4,863 allocated per FTE student representing a 19 percent drop from fiscal year 2003 as measured in constant dollars (State Higher Education Finance Report, 2009). When it

NEW DIRECTIONS FOR HIGHER EDUCATION, no. 151, Fall 2010 © Wiley Periodicals, Inc.
Published online in Wiley Online Library (wileyonlinelibrary.com) • DOI: 10.1002/he.399

comes to higher education support per $1,000 of personal income, Rhode Island's $3.86 in calendar year 2007 ranked it forty-seventh among the states, a decline from $5.70 in 2001 (forty-third) and $10.33 in 1981 (thirty-first) (Postsecondary Education Opportunity, 2009).

These figures comparing state funding have a lag time of two years. In that period, unemployment in Rhode Island skyrocketed to 12.9 percent (Bureau of Labor Statistics, 2009), and budget cuts continue to shrink allocations for non-entitlement programs. The state's 2009 budget cut $3 million from the revised 2008 budget allocation to the Rhode Island Higher Education Assistance Authority, which awards need-based aid to the state's college students (Rhode Island State Budget Executive Summary, FY 2009–2010, 2009). The state budget provides $6.3 million for grant aid—$400,000 less than it did in 1983 (Jordan, 2009a). Steve Maurano, Rhode Island's interim commissioner for higher education, said the recession combined with tuition increases necessitated by budget cuts means that money will be spread thinner. Although state funding may remain stagnant, total grant aid for needy Rhode Island students may decline next year because the state used more proceeds than planned from a college-savings plan run by the authority this year to compensate for the rising demand.

Despite the funding trends for public higher education in the state, measures of educational and economic outcomes in Rhode Island are mixed. This could be attributed to the state's strong private higher education system. Although it ranked forty-third among states for expenditures on public higher education institutions as a percentage of state product in 2006, Rhode Island ranked third by the same measure for private institutions (Postsecondary Education Opportunity, 2009). Nearly 33 percent of the state's population held at least a bachelor's degree in 2006, eleventh best in the nation. Despite high unemployment figures, Rhode Island does better than average in measures of poverty rates, per capita income, low-income college participation (Postsecondary Education Opportunity, 2009) and completion rates (The National Center for Public Policy in Higher Education, 2008).

A closer look at the trends, however, reveals cause for concern. Although Rhode Island ranked seventeenth in low-income college participation rate in 2007–2008 at 29.2 percent, that measure was down from a fourth-in-the-nation 42.3 percent in 1996–1997 (Postsecondary Education Opportunity, 2009). Likewise, data to measure the chances a high school freshman has of being enrolled in college at age 19 show Rhode Island ranked thirty-sixth in 2006, down from eighth in 1996. The percentage declined from 46.4 to 39.9 in that time (Postsecondary Education Opportunity, 2009). Rhode Island ranked dead last among states in the percentage of dependent Pell Grant recipients at its public universities (23.2 percent) in 2007–2008 (Postsecondary Education Opportunity, 2009). Though it ranked nineteenth in state need-based aid to cover Pell Grant recipients, its rank was down from fourth in 1986–1987 (Postsecondary Education

Opportunity, 2009). These trends are more alarming when data about the state's future high school graduates are examined. Less than 21 percent of students in fourth to ninth grade in the state qualified for free or reduced-price lunch in the 1987–1988 school year. That percentage increased to 36.4 in 1998–1999 and to 40.2 percent in 2007–2008 (Postsecondary Education Opportunity, 2009).

Robert Carothers, president of the University of Rhode Island (URI) from 1991 until his retirement earlier this year, said he heard politicians tout the importance of higher education to the state throughout his tenure, as appropriations decreased each year (personal communication, December 7, 2009). Not adjusting for inflation, the state allocates as much to URI now as it did in 1998, he said. And the percentage of the university's operating budget consisting of state support has declined from twenty-five to ten over the past eighteen years. Carothers began arguing a few years ago that the university should become private and predicts state funding will be nonexistent by 2012: "Public higher education statewide lost twenty-five million dollars last year and the university's share of that is about seventeen million. That's just in one year, so we're down now to fifty-five million and they're talking mid-year, another four million. So, you know, at a certain point in time it's not worth the aggravation."

Jack Warner, Rhode Island's higher education commissioner from 2002 to 2009, said he could see problems coming before the recession. Higher education received small gains in state funding in 2003, 2004, and 2005. By 2006 the appropriations started to slip, and with a Republican governor and large Democratic majority in the state legislature there was little collaboration about finding solutions to the budget problems "so the result of that was the discretionary areas of spending took a disproportionate hit." In recent years the state has saved money through consolidation. The state consolidated legal and human resources administrative functions across campuses, Warner said, and cut requirements for bachelor's and associate's degrees statewide. Bachelor's degrees went from 136 credits in some cases to a limit of 120 to 124. Associate's degree programs were downsized from eighty-plus credits to sixty. Warner said these moves addressed time to degree concerns and held down the total cost of higher education for students dealing with annual per-credit tuition hikes of nearly 10 percent. The state also eliminated fifty-six programs on its campuses in recent years, cutting programs that failed to graduate five students for two consecutive years, Warner said. It is now in the process of reviewing programs that did not graduate ten students for two consecutive years.

The recent decline in funding, from an already relatively poor position, leaves Maurano wondering if the state is reaching a breaking point in its ability to fill its duty of educating the state's students. "We're starting to run the risk of not being able to serve our students as well as we'd like to . . . one of the problems with that is we have a population that votes with their feet." The ability of the state's public higher education institutions to market

NEW DIRECTIONS FOR HIGHER EDUCATION • DOI: 10.1002/he

themselves to students is important, as Rhode Island is a net importer of college students and URI enrolls a relatively high percentage of students from out of state—nearly 40 percent (University of Rhode Island Office of Institutional Research, 2009). Despite these fears, the state's public colleges have never been more popular. Enrollment in the state's public higher education system this fall reached a record-high 43,412 students, Maurano said. He credits this to the lower tuition rates public higher education institutions offer to in-state students. This advantage is of particular importance during a recession, which started earlier in Rhode Island than most other states.

The state has thus far been able to deal with the cuts largely through tuition increases and hiring freezes, Maurano said. As of this November, Maurano said, the state higher education system had between 330 and 340 vacant positions as compared to 75 to 100 vacancies under normal circumstances. For a system that Maurano describes as "busting at the seams," it creates a dangerous dynamic. "We're walking a tightrope here because clearly a decline in personnel means that we are less able to provide some services to students and faculty more readily than we would be able to if we had a more full complement of staff." He added that there is frustration from universities that "just at the time that we have our greatest demand we have the fewest amount of resources in recent memory to be able to service that demand." But unlike in other states, such as Virginia, universities have not used declining state support to garner more autonomy. In fact, Maurano said the budget crisis has created just the opposite effect: "Normally they [universities] do have a lot more autonomy here. But we were, sort of, politely threatened by the current administration of the state that they wanted to approve all of our hiring. And as an autonomous system we were very much opposed to that and we fought that. The way we got them off our back was we said, 'We'll make sure the commissioner's office will provide a screen on the institutional hiring and so that way you guys won't have to do it'" (personal communication, November 15, 2009).

Massachusetts

Massachusetts is not experiencing the severe unemployment problems of its neighbor to the south, but higher education has been affected by the economic crisis. Double-digit cuts in state funding at the public flagship, University of Massachusetts-Amherst (UMass-Amherst), have prompted a plan by the university's chancellor to drastically increase enrollment of higher-paying out-of-state students (Jan, 2009). The state already ranked in the bottom ten in the nation in two measures of public support for higher education—as a percentage of personal income and by population—before additional cuts to higher education last year (Schworm, 2008). When adjusting for inflation, state spending on higher education decreased by more than $555 million between fiscal year 2001 and fiscal year 2010 (Massachusetts Budget, 2009). Higher education support per $1,000 of personal income for calendar year 2007 was actually lower than Rhode Island's. The state ranked last in the nation in spending on public higher education as a percentage of gross state product (Postsecondary Education Opportunity, 2009). But Massachusetts' wealth and its strong system of private education mitigate these shortcomings. It ranks fourth in the nation in per capita income and is first in the nation in expenditures of private institutions of higher education as a proportion of state product (Postsecondary Education Opportunity, 2009). And though appropriations have fallen, the $7,381 spent per full-time equivalent (FTE) student in public institutions in 2008 was slightly above the national average and about $2,500 more than Rhode Island (State Higher Education Finance Report, 2009). As might be expected, given its relative wealth, Massachusetts ranked second in the nation in percentage of residents with at least bachelor's degrees in 2008 (43.2 percent) and is ranked sixth in the most recent figures on a high school freshman's chances for college by age 19—though that's down from second in 1998 (Postsecondary Education Opportunity, 2009).

Massachusetts does not face the same demographic challenges as Rhode Island, either. The percentage of elementary and secondary students in Massachusetts qualifying for free or reduced lunch has increased 3 percent in the past decade to 30.9 percent—lower than all but two states (Postsecondary Education Opportunity, 2009). The state unemployment rate is only 8.9 percent (Bureau of Labor Statistics, 2009). The low-income college participation rate in Massachusetts has actually improved since the beginning of the decade by 3 percent, to 36.1 percent—fifth in the nation (Postsecondary Education Opportunity). Private four-year not-for-profit institutions actually enroll a higher percentage of Pell Grant recipients—32.1, second in the nation—than public higher education institutions—22.6, forty-fifth in the nation (Postsecondary Education Opportunity, 2009). Given the relatively high percentage of low-income students enrolled in the state's private institutions and the fact that public institutions enroll only about 41 percent of college students in the state (State Higher Education Executive Officers State Facts, 2009), do funding cuts to public higher education present a serious access problem? UMass-Amherst Chancellor Robert Holub thinks they do because he expects most of the future enrollment growth in the state to be in the public sector (personal communication, November 20, 2009):

> You have a president right now who wants us to be leading the country once again in producing advance degrees. That's going to be very difficult if you have states disinvesting in public higher education. Because you're not going to get it from the privates. Privates are not going to increase their capacity by enough and they don't have a model that's sustainable enough to be able to reach the goals that the Obama administration has set forth. Harvard isn't going to double its undergraduate population. But the publics in the state of Massachusetts could [with additional funding] very easily double the number of students who are going to receive either associate degrees, or B.A., or B.S. degrees.

NEW DIRECTIONS FOR HIGHER EDUCATION • DOI: 10.1002/he

The lack of funding has led to hiring freezes and administrative consolidations on the UMass-Amherst campus. Holub said combining positions in the provost's and chancellor's offices saved hundreds of thousands of dollars and consolidating programs in the school's College of Natural Resources and the Environment, and its College of Natural Science and Mathematics saved about $500,000 with more savings to come. Holub expects mid-year state budget cuts in January with more reductions a near certainty next year when public higher education in the state is expected to face a "funding cliff." That cliff is due to the fact that more than $150 million in federal stimulus money for higher education in the state, meant to cover three fiscal years, was used up almost entirely in the current budget, according to Massachusetts State Commissioner of Higher Education Richard Freeland (personal communication, December 3, 2009). Even with the influx of federal money, Freeland said, state colleges and the community college system used several cost-cutting measures in recent years, including layoffs. Like Warner's concerns about Rhode Island, Freeland said the community college system in Massachusetts is experiencing difficulties handling enrollment growth. The system has reduced costs, he said, by replacing "full-time faculty with part-time faculty so there's been a tremendous shift of the instructional program. . . . Across the community colleges, two-thirds of our classes are taught by part-time faculty."

Support for capital expansion to take on enrollment growth was also hampered by the recession. A proposed $2.2 billion bond bill for capital improvements on the state's campuses was cut back after the 2008 economic collapse "severely truncated" the state's ability to borrow, Freeland said, while expansion and renovation on the state's campuses "has been quite neglected on the state level."

In addition to cuts, Massachusetts public higher education institutions have compensated for the declining revenues by raising tuition and fees for in-state residents across all three systems. In constant dollars, tuition and fees at UMass-Amherst went from $6,336 in 2001–2002 (122 percent of the national average for state flagships) to $10,234 in 2008–2009 (137 percent of the national average) (Postsecondary Education Opportunity, 2009). The average in-state tuition and fee rates for institutions in the state college system jumped from $4,006 (97 percent of the national average) to $6,917 (118 percent of the national average) in that same period of time and the community college system increased tuition and fees from $2,771 to $3,682— 135 percent of the national community college average (Postsecondary Education Opportunity, 2009). The stimulus allowed the UMass system to avoid a 15 percent hike in tuition and fees this year, knocking $1,100 off of a $1,500 increase (Nicas, 2009).

Tuition and fee charges for out-of-state students are $23,229 at UMass-Amherst this year, more than double the charges for in-state students. With only 20 percent of students enrolled at the university from out of state (University of Massachusetts Fact Sheets, 2009), Holub sees an opportunity to grow enrollment and make up for lost revenues by increasing that percentage. The number of high school graduates in the state is expected to decline sharply through 2014–2015 (Western Interstate Commission for Higher Education, 2008) so Holub said plans to grow enrollment by 15 percent by recruiting out-of-state students will not affect the university's mission to educate students in the state. "If we're going to grow the campus by a couple of thousand then we'll grow it with out-of-state students since they'll help to pay for the students who are from Massachusetts," he said.

Recruiting out-of-state students who have less-expensive options at public universities in their home states is easier said than done. Michael Thomas, president and chief executive officer of the New England Board of Higher Education, questions the practicality of the strategy: "They can talk about wanting to increase the number of out-of-state students but I think they'll probably find an impediment in terms of both public opinion and legislative support for that. And then I'm just not—the question is how many of those students they would get paying full freight?" (personal communication, November 16, 2009).

Holub said his university remains dedicated to its mission of providing education to Massachusetts students but public universities in general are increasingly looked upon as a private good as their sources for funding shift. In keeping with that philosophy, he needs to look at ways to diversify revenues, he said.

Michael Goodman, chair of the department of public policy at UMass-Dartmouth, agrees with Holub's assessment of the state as an unreliable partner. "You hear people say, 'We used to be state funded, now we're state assisted, and we're on our way to being state located'. . . . Public higher education needs to be released and enabled to be a little bit more entrepreneurial" (personal communication, November 10, 2009).

Possible Solutions and Analysis

Massachusetts and Rhode Island appear likely to remain in the bottom tier of states in many measures of support for public higher education. While declining public funding of higher education is a national trend, historical inequities between the public and private higher education sectors have a way of perpetuating themselves. In assessing both states, Warner said getting a robust appropriation is a challenge in part because of political dynamics: "In Massachusetts, for example, the majority of legislators graduate from Suffolk and BU and BC and Northeastern and those places. Privates don't want you to get a large appropriation because it will result in a low tuition that competes with them—unfairly in their view."

Raising tuition sticker prices—so as to advertise a more "fair" market price that's more in line with private universities—is one way state institutions could help address budget shortfalls. Need-based tuition discounting could then address access issues for low-income students, but universities would have to carefully balance a limited budget with concerns about their place in the market, their access mission, and institutional prestige. And there's the matter of accountability. State funding still provides enough to the operating budget that concerns by politicians and the public must be considered. In a sense, public higher education institutions are now caught between two worlds—they receive less state funding than they once enjoyed but there's still enough state buy-in to limit their freedom. "I don't know that the legislators would be willing to give up that control because certainly raising the retail price would have political ramifications, right?" Goodman asked.

Adopting a high-tuition, high-aid model—skewed heavily toward need— is one of three ways Tom Mortenson believes higher education can be saved (personal communication, December 4, 2009). A senior scholar at the Pell Institute for the Study of Opportunity in Higher Education, Mortenson is convinced that the system of funding for higher education is broken. Another solution he offered included a nationalization of higher education, where tuition is set at an expected family contribution and resources are pooled and then reallocated to the college. A sharp increase in taxes on the wealthy would be another way to address the issue, he said. Mortenson admits that none of the solutions are likely to get any political support, but he estimates higher education would need an influx of $40 to $50 billion to properly address the problem of access being caused by declining support and rising tuition costs. "The situation is as bad as it's ever been," he said. "There's no incremental, marginal, sort of, politically neutral kind of answer."

Mortenson also thinks universities need to abandon the student amenities arms race to cut costs. Decisions to grow out-of-state enrollment result in states wasting money luring students from other states while taking the focus off of needy students. He said twenty-seven states are increasing their percentage of non-resident students while decreasing their share of Pell Grant students. "Higher education, left to its own, would kill the country," he said. As demographics change, he said, these practices will result in the further stratification of classes and cause the United States to lose national competitiveness. Policy makers in both Massachusetts and Rhode Island share Mortenson's beliefs about the benefits of higher education, but their solutions often fall into "incremental, marginal, sort of politically neutral" category. "Clearly we're a system in great peril. We're a state in great crisis," Maurano said of Rhode Island. "And I don't personally see any way out in the near term." Thomas said governors in both states believe in the importance of higher education but lamented that "right now, it's just an issue of constraints." Holub laments a lack of "some kind of a national will" to better support higher education.

Increasing educational attainment is a proven method of improving an area's economic health and is positively correlated with a number of measures of social well-being. In short, the areas that could most benefit from improved access to higher education can least afford increasing allocations to public higher education. And while higher education has more alternative funding sources—and is relying on them more each year—the main alternative source to state funding—tuition—relies on wealth from students or their families. For these reasons, it seems that Massachusetts is clearly better equipped to turn around its record for higher education support. As Warner pointed out, Rhode Island does not have much on which to anchor its economy, and state budgets will continue to be strained by other obligations. And while Rhode Island is a net importer of students, many leave the state, he said, due to lack of jobs. Given the dynamics of this downward-spiraling system, Mortenson's calls for radical change make sense. In explaining the need for national political will to address the problem, Holub pointed to the leading role the federal government played in past expansion of higher education, such as the post–World War II growth spurred by the G.I. Bill and federal research dollars that flowed to universities after Sputnik.

If Southern New England is going to continue to prosper, it's clear that its public universities will have to play a major role, aided by state support and wise decisions on the campus level. Whether that will happen in time to turn around local economies, prepare a new generation of workers, and educate a changing pool of students is less certain. The higher education funding problems in Southern New England are a microcosm for the entire country. Many of the issues are the same—a dearth of resources and excess needs combined with the ability of higher education to find other resources has led to cuts at the same time politicians are touting higher education's role as an economic engine. But the fact that Massachusetts and Rhode Island already spent so little on public higher education and the historical importance of higher education to the region's prosperity might mean that the fall will be faster and harder in the two states absent swift and substantial change.

References

Bureau of Labor Statistics. "Unemployment Rates for States." Washington, D.C.: Bureau of Labor Statistics, 2009. Retrieved December 1, 2009, from http://www.bls.gov/web/laumstrk.htm

Courturier, L., and Cunningham, A. "Convergence: Trends Threatening to Narrow College Opportunity in America." Quincy, Mass.: The Nellie Mae Education Foundation, 2006. Retrieved November 4, 2009 from http://www.ihep.org/assets/files/publications/a-f/Convergence.pdf

Fain, P. "Less for More." *The New York Times*, November 1, 2009, p. 20.

Jan, T. "UMass to Recruit from the Outside; 15% Enrollment Increase Sought." *The Boston Globe*, October 11, 2009, p. 1.

Jordan, J. "State Scholarships for College Are Shrinking." *The Providence Journal*, June 23, 2009a, Local, p.1.

Jordan, J. "Board Votes to Increase Tuition at State Colleges." *The Providence Journal*, October 6, 2009b, p. 1.

Massachusetts Budget and Policy Center. "Comparisons of Past Year Spending." Boston: Massachusetts Budget and Policy Center, 2009. Retrieved November 29, 2009, from http://browser.massbudget.org/CompareVersionsHistoric.aspx
The National Center for Public Policy in Higher Education. "Measuring Up 2008." San Jose, Calif.: The National Center for Public Policy in Higher Education, 2008. Retrieved November 26, 2009, from http://measuringup2008.highereducation.org/
Nicas, J. "For Umass Students, A Welcome Financial Relief; Undergraduates to Get $1,100 Rebate. *The Boston Globe*, August 8, 2009, p. 1.
Postsecondary Education Opportunity. "State Reports." Oskaloosa, Iowa: Postsecondary Education Opportunity, 2009. Retrieved November 2, 2009, from http://www.postsecondary.org/peocountry.asp
Rhode Island State Budget Executive Summary, FY 2009–10. Providence, R.I.: State Budget Office, 2009. Retrieved December 2, 2009, from http://www.budget.ri.gov/Documents/CurrentFY/ExecutiveSummary/6_Education.pdf
Schworm, P. "State Behind in Spending on Public Colleges. Leaders Say More Is Needed to Compete." *The Boston Globe*, August 3, 2008, p. B1.
State Higher Education Executive Officers State Facts. Boulder, Colo.: State Higher Education Executive Officers, 2009. Retrieved November 14, 2009, from http://www.sheeo.org/sqf/sqf.htm
State Higher Education Finance Report, FY 2008. Boulder, Colo.: State Higher Education Executive Officers, 2009. Retrieved November 14, 2009, from http://sheeo.org/finance/shef_fy08.pdf
University of Massachusetts Fact Sheets. Amherst, Mass.: Office of Institutional Research, 2009. Retrieved December 1, 2009, from http://www.umass.edu/oapa/ publications/factsheets/student_charges/FS_chg_01.pdf
University of Rhode Island Office of Institutional Research. "URI Facts, Fall 2009." Kingston, R.I.: University of Rhode Island Office of Institutional Research, 2009. Retrieved December 1, 2009, from http://www.uri.edu/ir/
Western Interstate Commission for Higher Education. "Knocking at the College Door: Projections of High School Projections of High School Graduates by State and Race/Ethnicity." Boulder, Colo.: Western Interstate Commission for Higher Education, 2008. Retrieved December 5, 2009, from http://wiche.edu/info/publications/knocking_complete_book.pdf

GREGORY ESPOSITO *is a 2010 graduate of the Harvard Graduate School of Education. Previously, he was a reporter with* The Roanoke Times *and covered higher education.*

NEW DIRECTIONS FOR HIGHER EDUCATION • DOI: 10.1002/he

5

The transition of women's colleges into coeducational institutions presents fundamental issues and sensitive dynamics.

Tough Questions Facing Women's Colleges

Sara Kratzok

Since their creation in the latter part of the nineteenth century, women's colleges in America have undergone many significant changes. In 1960, over 230 women's colleges were in operation; over the next forty years more than 75 percent chose to admit men or shut their doors entirely (Miller-Bernal, 2006a). This chapter will shed light on the dilemmas facing women's colleges when pondering coeducation. I will look specifically to Lesley College's decision about coeducation as a case study that reveals the challenges facing many single-sex institutions. Underlying this analysis is one central question: What does the future hold for women's colleges?

Women's Colleges: A Long Tradition

In recent years, many women's colleges have had to weigh the proven benefits of single-sex education against lagging applications and falling revenue. According to research commissioned by the Women's College Coalition, graduates of women's colleges are more likely to receive degrees in the traditionally male-dominated fields of science and engineering. Women's college alumna are also more likely to graduate than their counterparts at coed schools and tend to have higher self-esteem (Women's College Coalition, 2009). The National Survey of Student Engagement (NSSE), comparing the satisfaction of students at women's colleges to female students at coed institutions, found that students at women's colleges felt more supported on campus and made "greater gains in college" (Kinzie and others, 2007, p. 145). Furthermore, they concluded that women's colleges were effective in providing students with academic challenges and support, and as such should serve as exemplars to all institutions of higher education (Kinzie and

NEW DIRECTIONS FOR HIGHER EDUCATION, no. 151, Fall 2010 © Wiley Periodicals, Inc.
Published online in Wiley Online Library (wileyonlinelibrary.com) • DOI: 10.1002/he.400

others, 2007). Despite the findings in support of single-sex education, the largest problem facing these institutions today is the pipeline. No longer the sole option for young women, research has indicated that only about 3 percent of high school females will even consider attending women's colleges, largely due to social concerns (Calefati, 2009). Currently, many women's colleges are faced with choosing between their identities and their enrollments.

The Push for Coeducation

In October 2004, Wells College, a women's college located in the Finger Lakes region of upstate New York (Aurora), announced that after 136 years as a single-sex institution, it would go coed the following fall (Moore, 2004). Administrators stated that low enrollment numbers and struggling finances motivated the decision. A familiar sentiment among women's colleges who have made the difficult decision to admit men is "coed or dead." According to Wells President Lisa Marsh Ryerson that was certainly the case on her campus (Moore, 2004).

Wells had examined multiple options for improving enrollment and finances, and, at what Miller-Bernal (2006b) refers to as "the last minute," coeducation was pitched to the trustees of the college. The faculty agreed that coeducation options should be examined, and professional consultants were brought in to ease the transition. Less than a year after coeducation was first seriously proposed, the trustees voted to admit men (Miller-Bernal, 2006b). The response among Wells students was swift and strong. Although earlier campus research implied that many Wells students had enrolled *despite* the institution's status as a women's college, many students expressed feelings of betrayal (Miller-Bernal, 2006b). Students staged sit-ins and took over an administrative building for more than a week, and some even sued the college, but the plan for coeducation went into effect (Moore, 2004). By 2007, applications to the college had increased by nearly 300 percent, and Wells saw its largest enrollment since 1972 (Sunkin, 2007). Today, Wells is 30 percent male and doesn't foresee reaching gender parity among the student body (Wells College External Relations Office, 2008; Sunkin, 2007).

Regis College, located in suburban Weston, Massachusetts, decided to go coed in the fall of 2006. Founded as a Catholic college in 1927, Regis had considered admitting men several times in its history (Noonan, 2007). By 2006, college administrators assessed that to be able to fund much-needed improvements, as well as salaries for a growing faculty, the college would need to expand enrollment quickly; administrators felt that admitting men was the only way to accomplish that goal (Bombardieri and Jan, 2006). Thus, the college was willing to take on the additional initial cost of admitting men, which they estimated at up to $1 million per year for several years, to reach long-term financial stability. The money would go to funding male athletic teams (a requirement of Title IX that specifies gender equity in sports), as well as hiring male admissions officers and overhauling their marketing materials (Bombardieri and Jan, 2006).

Although students expressed sadness over the college's decision, the sentiment on campus seemed to be that it would be better to admit men than shut down, once again echoing the "coed or dead" adage (Bombardieri and Jan, 2006). According to Regis faculty member Susan Tammaro, there was also division between older alumnae who seemed to support the college's decision, and younger alums who expressed outrage (Powers, 2006). This seems to support an assertion by David Strauss, a Principal Consultant for the Art and Science Group, who has worked with several women's colleges on the topic of coeducation. Strauss posits that alums who have struggled (and frequently failed) to convince their own daughters to consider the benefits of a single-sex college tend to be a bit more understanding about coeducation than their younger counterparts (personal communication, November 24, 2009).

In some ways, it may be becoming easier for women's colleges to make such decisions as they see so many of their peers accepting difficult realities and enrolling male students. Regis admitted sixty men for the fall of 2007 and is now roughly 14 percent male (Noonan, 2007; National Center for Educational Statistics, 2008; Regis College Admissions Office, 2009). Much like Wells, sentiment on Regis campus is that the college will always be predominantly female, but with the acceptance of men will now be viable for years to come (Bombardieri and Jan, 2006).

Other women's colleges have seriously considered coeducation but chose to remain single-sex institutions. In 1990, the trustees of Mills College (Oakland, Calif.) voted to admit men due to mounting financing concerns but within two weeks rescinded their decision (Sheldon, 2006). Students and faculty essentially shut down the campus due to boycotts and ultimately convinced the trustees to reconsider and hold onto the identity the college had created over the previous 138 years. The pressure of several important constituencies banding together against coeducation made all the difference in the college's future.

The results of Mills's failed coeducation attempt were largely positive. Once students and faculty finished celebrating their victory, administrators got to work to find new ways to ensure the college's future as a single-sex institution. Within a few years of the decision, many administrators had been replaced, creating an "atmosphere of optimism and energy" on campus (Sheldon, 2006). The college put a new emphasis on recruiting and attracting students and for the first time created a marketing department. Thanks to this and other measures, the college reported applications had increased 82 percent by 2005 (Jaschik, 2005).

Finances are often cited as the factor that divides the women's colleges who will be pushed to consider coeducation or closure and those who will not. Wellesley College (Wellesley, Mass.) is often considered the least vulnerable to coeducation, largely because the institution has the largest endowment of any women's college (Miller-Bernal and Poulson, 2006). Wellesley last considered coeducation in 1971 when a "Commission on the Future of the College" was created to make recommendations for the institution's future. The commission voted 9 to 4 in favor of coeducation, but the Board of Trustees rejected the proposal (Tarantino, 2009). The trustees felt that despite the movement on campus and in the country for increased gender equity, there was still an important place for women's colleges. At this time, the college has no plans to reconsider the coeducation question (Tarantino, 2009).

Wellesley remains one of five of the original Seven Sisters colleges to continue to operate as single-sex institutions. Along with Mount Holyoke (South Hadley, Mass.), Bryn Mawr (Bryn Mawr, Penn.), Smith (Northampton, Mass.), and Barnard (New York), the sister colleges, as they are now known, "have continued to meet to discuss issues of common concern, such as institutional goals, admissions, financial aid, and curriculum matters" (Mount Holyoke College Office of Communications, 2007). These schools have made names for themselves outside of their identity as women's colleges; they appeal to students for a variety of reasons other than their single-sex nature. In doing so, they have effectively recognized the new market for women's colleges. Strauss, the consultant who "specializes in market-informed strategy for colleges and universities in the non-profit sector," has worked with a number of women's colleges trying to position themselves to remain single-sex (Art & Science Group, LLC, 2009). In a recent conversation, Strauss noted that the most successful women's colleges have succeeded by virtue of distinguishing themselves in some way other than their single-sex identity. In fact, surveys conducted by the Art and Science Group found that as many as 60 percent of the students who elect to attend women's colleges matriculated despite the fact that the college was single-sex (D. Strauss, personal communication, November 24, 2009).

Case Study: Lesley College

Located in Cambridge, Massachusetts, Lesley College was founded in 1909 by kindergarten teacher Edith Lesley, who saw the need for a school that would educate female kindergarten and early elementary teachers. Lesley became known for its four-year teacher education program and by 1954 was offering a master's degree program in elementary education. Evolving with the changing times, Lesley has offered graduate programs in a variety of areas linked to social justice and public service. From their start, Lesley's graduate programs were coeducational, and in 1998 the college merged with the Art Institute of Boston (AIB).

In 2004, the undergraduate college made the pivotal decision to admit men (Lesley University Archives, 2009). According to Carol Streit, Lesley University's former vice president of enrollment, the success of the merger opened the door to educating men at the undergraduate level. Male AIB students moved into what had once been single-sex dorms, and all of the university's co-curricular activities became coed. Liberal arts classes at Lesley were opened to AIB students, so a few men at a time began to enroll in the all-female courses. Lesley's single-sex culture began to be completely transformed (personal communication, November 19, 2009).

Streit noted in a 2005 op-ed that the decision of coeducation was largely born out of thoughtful reflection on the institution's history and mission. As a college committed to training teachers and public service professionals, Lesley officials felt they could no longer justify closing their doors to men, knowing the profound shortage of men in such fields (Streit, 2005). Lesley President Margaret McKenna also emphasized the paucity of high school females interested in single-sex education and the college's desire to increase the size and caliber of its applicant pool (Emery, 2004). Prior to the decision to admit men, Lesley's applications had largely been flat, and the college had reached an acceptance rate of 80 percent (Emery, 2004; Russell, 2004). At the time of the decision, much emphasis was placed on the fact that Lesley was financially stable (Russell, 2004).

In preparation for the advent of coeducation on campus, a consulting group worked with the university to re-brand the institution. In 2005 the new tag line "Wake up the World" was publicly announced (Doncaster, 2005). A college press release highlighted the college's focus on social justice careers (Doncaster, 2005). The college found much success with its new brand, which begs the question, could enrollments have increased as a direct result of the new marketing efforts without the college deciding to admit men? Lesley officials acknowledge that older marketing materials did not accurately capture the college's mission. "Wake up the World" was the first centralized campaign the college had ever attempted (Gatlin, 2005).

The university also realized that coeducation required major overhauls in the curriculum to both improve the educational offerings and attract male students. Debra Kocar, Lesley College's Director of Admissions, noted that majors in business management, global studies, and communications were all modified to be more appealing to young men. A political science track was added to the global studies major, and sports management became a part of the business management course offerings. Within the teacher education field of study, a secondary school track for science teachers was added, and the math and biology teaching programs were expanded. Additionally, internships became a much larger component of the Lesley education. According to Kocar, the college "realized that [it] had the opportunity to be a small institution offering internships in a city environment without religious affiliation—this was a huge marketing opportunity" (personal communication, November 24, 2009).

To make these sweeping changes to the curriculum, Lesley's faculty needed to sign-off. Concerned about male students feeling marginalized, the faculty spent a year having monthly meetings to discuss pedagogy. Faculty members pored over articles about the way young men learn best, and their

NEW DIRECTIONS FOR HIGHER EDUCATION • DOI: 10.1002/he

findings helped inform new teaching methods that were meant to ease the transition into coed classrooms (D. Kocar, personal communication, November 24, 2009). The faculty research and training illustrates how one of the most important college constituencies whole-heartedly embraced coeducation.

Lesley College alumnae also expressed concern and disappointment when the college announced their decision. Despite focus groups and discussions with alums, some still felt angry and believed the college was moving in the wrong direction. Streit noted that college administrators believed it was very important to align themselves with Lesley graduates, and they learned that lesson from the mistakes of other women's colleges that had alienated alums when they went coed. College leaders tried to involve the alumnae council to ensure there was clear messaging about the college's decision (C. Streit, personal communication November 19, 2009). Despite the best efforts of administrators, some alumnae were still deeply hurt by the decision, and as a result the admissions office chose not to involve any Lesley graduates in student recruiting events for several years (D. Kocar, personal communication, November 24, 2009).

Other recruitment efforts also changed once the university decided to move ahead with coeducation plans. Three male admissions counselors were hired to join the formerly all-female admissions office. Admissions officers also began to reach out to high schools that they had never visited before. Kocar also reports that many parents of young men came to recruiting events with questions and concerns about their sons attending a formerly single-sex college. It soon became clear to Kocar and others in the admissions office that it was necessary to have male students on admissions panels as soon as possible to share their perspectives on the Lesley experience. At recruiting events, admissions officers played up the "trailblazing" aspect of being one of the first men at Lesley (D. Kocar, personal communication, November 24, 2009).

Another way that Lesley attracted male students was through the strategic use of institutional aid. Carol Streit noted that for the first few years of coed enrollment the college offered preferential aid packages to men to encourage their attendance (2009). Streit justified leveraging financial aid to attract male students as part of increasing campus diversity and responding to the institution's enrollment needs. Previously, the college had experimented in offering steeper tuition discounts to students of color in an effort to increase diversity, and simply saw the use of preferential packaging for men as an extension of such tactics. Consultants assured administrators that if they kept their new enrollment strategy in place, after the fourth year of coeducation they would begin to see returns on their investments in marketing, admissions, and financial aid (C. Streit, personal communication November 19, 2009).

Once classes began in September 2005, several more unintended consequences of the college's decision to admit men came to the forefront on campus. Academically, students acknowledged that they appreciated having the diversity of thought that male students brought to class discussions (S. Chin, personal e-mail communication, December 3, 2009; L. Skillin, personal e-mail communication, December 4, 2009). However, as Skillin put it, some professors "were so focused to make sure the male student felt equal and not outnumbered that it felt like they ignored the rest of the class, which were female students." Thomas Morgan, a Lesley College graduate from the class of 2009, and one of the first men who enrolled at Lesley, remembers that some female students seemed hesitant to trust male students at first, and accusations flew around campus that male students had been held to lower admissions standards. Some female students made Morgan feel as though he "was more there symbolically than to participate in education" (personal communication, December 2, 2009).

After a while, Morgan says the need for male students to prove themselves to their female peers faded, but it was clear that some young women on campus felt that the presence of men was negatively affecting their college experience (T. Morgan, personal communication, December 2, 2009). Skillin recalls that a number of her classmates transferred to other colleges as a direct result of the coeducation decision, and other students chose to commute to campus rather than live in coed dormitories (personal e-mail communication, December 4, 2009). Administrators observed that women on campus seemed to become more aware of their appearances in the coed environment—gone were the days of going to class in pajamas (D. Kocar, personal communication, November 24, 2009). Morgan also "got the feeling that women felt ignored as men were being pampered," which further contributed to the rift between male and female students (personal communication, December 2, 2009).

According to Kocar, living and working together was difficult for Lesley students during the first few years of coeducation. Campus housing saw a fair amount of conflict as some dorms went coed and others remained single-sex. Male students often felt outnumbered and complained about female students dominating common space in the dorms. Kocar did point out that after a few years of coeducation "the energy on campus started to change," and many of the initial issues began to work themselves out. With each new class that included male students, the men on campus began to be seen for their contributions to the college, frequently through athletics and leadership, rather than for how their presence altered what had been the college's most defining characteristic (D. Kocar, personal communication, November 24, 2009).

From the viewpoint of Lesley administrators, coeducation improved the college in many ways. Streit remarked that "all quality measures are closer to being met now . . . average SAT scores and GPAs have all increased" since coeducation began (personal communication, November 19, 2009). The college's selectivity has also increased; in 2008 Lesley accepted 65 percent of its applicants, down 15 percent since before the school went coed ("Best Colleges 2010," 2009). Lesley has also been able to attract a more diverse group of students, not only in terms of gender, but in geography and interests as well

(C. Streit, personal communication, November 19, 2009). Today the college is 22 percent male with the hope of reaching 30 percent in the future (D. Kocar, personal communication, November 24, 2009). The overall goal of the college is to have a "healthy, rich population for students" but, much like Wells College, there are no plans for the male population to exceed more than 30 percent (D. Kocar, personal communication, November 24, 2009).

As for the first class of male students who entered Lesley, of the twenty-one who began as freshman only four graduated with the class of 2009 (D. Kocar, personal communication, November 24, 2009). Many of the students were members of the college's brand-new men's basketball team, and they expressed disappointment that they did not have more of a "typical" college experience. According to Kocar, some of the students specifically sought to transfer to other colleges with more-established athletic programs, while others were simply not "academically viable." Lesley may have experimented with admissions preferences for athletes a bit prematurely as they sought to recruit their first class with male students. It is also possible that social issues proved to be too challenging for some of the young men, just as they were for their female peers who also chose to transfer elsewhere.

Lessons from Lesley

While there may have been some initial missteps as Lesley College formed its identity as a coed institution, in many ways the transition was incredibly successful. Administrators and consultants thoroughly researched what other women's colleges had done well when becoming coed, and also what mistakes those colleges had made along the way (C. Streit, personal communication, November 19, 2009). With that in mind, Streit also feels that "the context and particulars of Lesley were crucial to [the] overall success." Kocar still advises other women's colleges grappling with the decision to go forward with it. She says, "Don't be afraid to do it . . . just make sure the students are at the center of the equation" (D. Kocar, personal communication, November 24, 2009).

Looking to the Future

With the current state of the economy, many colleges and universities are evaluating how to remain financially viable for the long-term. Women's colleges are particularly vulnerable, as many must contend with low enrollment numbers and low levels of admissions selectivity. As Miller-Bernal and Poulson (2006) put it, many women's colleges "no longer are what they once were—liberal arts colleges serving traditional-aged residential students. Instead the majority of women's colleges have adapted to changes in the marketplace by changing their curriculum, altering the ways they enroll students, and reaching out to different, often less academically prepared, population groups" (p. 376).

NEW DIRECTIONS FOR HIGHER EDUCATION • DOI: 10.1002/he

   While some women's college have become more nimble and adaptable as a result of changing demands, others have suffered and been forced to consider coeducation as the most reasonable way to quickly boost enrollment and revenue. The alternative for many schools is to become even less selective, and then potentially face low levels of student retention and high costs of remediation, if the caliber of academics offered on campus does not match the preparation of students.

   Women's colleges have proven benefits for female students, but should struggling schools choose coeducation to survive or shut their doors for all? Strauss feels that the key to remaining single-sex is having balance and knowing how to work against what is frequently seen as the burden of remaining single-sex. He predicts that in the future, some women's institutions will retain a small single-sex undergraduate college while growing coed programs for adult students. In that scenario, the only women's colleges to stay truly single-sex will be a small group of financially stable colleges that have distinguished themselves in some way to remain competitive with their coed peer institutions. The other option Strauss proposes is "some collective action on the part of women's colleges to try do what can be done to promote the positive appeal of women's colleges and blunt the negative stereotypes" that prevent many female students from enrolling. Short of those options he feels that there will be a continued erosion of the market for women's colleges (D. Strauss, personal communication, November 24, 2009).

   No women's college arrives at the decision to go coed lightly. All the colleges highlighted in this chapter thoughtfully examined their options, often with the help of private consultants, before making a final decision on coeducation. Administrators at Wells, Regis, Mills, Wellesley, and Lesley ultimately did what they felt was right for their campuses and constituencies, and all continue to operate to this day. Women's colleges have many difficulties they must overcome to compete with their coed peers, but hopefully as long as some members of the college-going population show a demand for women's colleges, such institutions will continue to thrive. It is likely that the future of women's colleges will play out as a survival of the fittest (or most endowed). For those colleges that do not survive as single-sex institutions, they should look to Lesley College and other schools that have successfully transitioned as examples of what to do next.

References

Art & Science Group, LLC. "Firm Overview." Retrieved November 18, 2009, from http://www.artsci.com/about_us/overview_marketing_university.aspx

"Best Colleges 2010." *U.S. News and World Report*, August 20, 2009. Retrieved December 6, 2009, from http://colleges.usnews.rankingsandreviews.com

Bombardieri, M., and Jan, T. "Regis College to Admit Men in '07." *The Boston Globe*, September 1, 2006. Retrieved November 18, 2009, from http://www.boston.com/news/local/massachusetts/articles/2006/09/01/regis_college_to_admit_men_in_07/

New Directions for Higher Education • DOI: 10.1002/he

Calefati, J. "The Changing Face of Women's Colleges." *U.S. News and World Report*, March 11, 2009. Retrieved December 4, 2009, from http://www.usnews.com/articles/education/2009/03/11/the-changing-face-of-womens-colleges.html

Doncaster, B. "Lesley University Launches Bold New Brand Identity." Cambridge, Mass.: Lesley University Office of Public Affairs, April 13, 2005. Retrieved November 18, 2009, from http://www.lesley.edu/news/press_releases/20050413branding.html

Emery, T. "One of Massachusetts' Last All-Women Colleges Soon Will Admit Men." *The Associated Press*, June 9, 2004. Retrieved November 18, 2009, from http://www.lexis nexis.com

Gatlin, G. "'Wake Up' Campaign Gives Lift to Lesley; Public Service Is the Focus as Applications Rise 150%." *The Boston Herald*, April 25, 2005. Retrieved November 18, 2009, from http://www.bostonherald.com

Jaschik, S. "Male Impact." *Inside Higher Ed*, July 19, 2005. Retrieved November 18, 2009, from http://www.insidehighered.com/layout/set/dialog/news/2005/07/19/men

Kinzie, J., and others. "Women Students at Coeducation and Women's Colleges: How Do Their Experiences Compare?" *The Journal of College Student Development*, March/April, 2007, 48(2), 145–165.

Lesley University Archives. "History." Cambridge, Mass.: Lesley University, April 24, 2009. Retrieved November 18, 2009, from http://www.lesley.edu/about/archive/his tory.html

Miller-Bernal, L. "Introduction: Changes in the Status and Function of Women's Colleges over Time." In L. Miller-Bernal and S. L. Poulson (eds.), *Challenged by Coeducation*. Nashville, Tenn.: Vanderbilt University Press, 2006a.

Miller-Bernal, L. "Wells College: The Transition to Coeducation Begins." In L. Miller-Bernal and S. L. Poulson (eds.), *Challenged by Coeducation*. Nashville, Tenn.: Vanderbilt University Press, 2006b.

Miller-Bernal, L., and Poulson, S. L. "The State of Women's Colleges Today." In L. Miller-Bernal and S. L. Poulson (eds.), *Challenged by Coeducation*. Nashville, Tenn.: Vanderbilt University Press, 2006.

Moore, M. T. "Women Rail Against College's Coed Plans." *USA Today*, December 12, 2004. Retrieved November 18, 2009, from http://www.usatoday.com/news/nation/2004-12-12-women-college_x.htm

Mount Holyoke College Office of Communications. "The Seven Sisters." South Hadley, Mass.: Mount Holyoke College, 2007, February 19, 2007. Retrieved December 4, 2009, from http://www. mtholyoke.edu/cic/about/12812.shtml

National Center for Education Statistics, Integrated Postsecondary Education Data System. Weston, Mass.: Regis College, 2008. Retrieved December 4, 2009 from http://nces.ed.gov/ipeds/ datacenter

Noonan, E. "Fresh-man: Arrival of Male Students at Regis Signals Change at Catholic College." *The Boston Globe*, July 8, 2007. Retrieved December 4, 2009, from http://www.boston.com/news/local/articles/2007/07/08/fresh_man_class/

Powers, E. "Rebellion Over Coeducation Plan." *Inside Higher Ed*, September 6, 2006. Retrieved December 4, 2009, from http://www.insidehighered.com/news/2006/09/06/coed

Regis College Admissions Office. "About Regis." Weston, Mass.: Regis College, 2009. Retrieved December 4, 2009 from http://www.regiscollege.edu/AboutRegis/default .aspx

Russell, J. "Lesley College to Admit Men Next Year." *The Boston Globe*, June 9, 2004. Retrieved November 18, 2009, from http://www.boston.com/news/local/articles/2004/06/09/lesley_college_to_admit_men_next_year/

Sheldon, M. "Revitalizing the Mission of a Women's College: Mills College in Oakland, California." In L Miller-Bernal and S. L. Poulson (eds.), *Challenged by Coeducation*. Nashville, Tenn.: Vanderbilt University Press, 2006.

Streit, C. "Going Coed at Lesley College." *University Business*, August 2005. Retrieved November 18, 2009, from http://www.universitybusiness.com/viewarticle.aspx?articleid=469

Sunkin, A. "Wells Enrollment Hits 35-Year High." *The Citizen*, August 31, 2007. Retrieved December 4, 2009, from http://www.auburnpub.com

Tarantino, M. "Forty Years Later: Wellesley's Decision to Stay–A Women's College Revisited." Wellesley, Mass.: Wellesley College Office of Public Affairs, February 27, 2009. Retrieved December 4, 2009, from http://www.wellesley.edu/PublicAffairs/Releases/2009/022709.html

Wells College External Relations Office. "Wells At a Glance." Aurora, N.Y.: *Wells College*, Nov. 12, 2008. Retrieved December 4, 2009, from http://www.wells.edu/at-a-glance/inbrief.htm

Women's College Coalition. "Research and Information." Hartford, Conn.: Women's College Coalition, 2009. Retrieved December 4, 2009, from http://www.womenscolleges.org/story/research

SARA KRATZOK is a recent graduate of the Ed.M in Higher Education program from the Harvard Graduate School of Education, 2010.

New Directions for Higher Education • DOI: 10.1002/he

6

Faculty can find even successful careers more stressful than they expected.

Stress in Senior Faculty Careers

Brendan C. Russell

According to the Carnegie Foundation, faculty job satisfaction has declined drastically over the past few decades at institutions of higher education (Shuster and Finkelstein, 2006). Researchers have also found that faculty satisfaction is critical to the vitality of colleges and universities (Clark, Corcoran, and Lewis, 1986; Farrell, 1983). Senior faculty members, defined here as those who have tenure, can significantly impact institutional vitality because they make up 50 percent of the professoriate (U.S. Department of Education, 2008). In addition, a recent study suggests that one disengaged senior faculty member can significantly damage an entire academic unit at a college or university (Huston, Norman, and Ambrose, 2007). Due to the potential for such negative effects, researchers have asked the following question: What factors affect senior faculty retention and attrition at institutions of higher education? I begin the following chapter by analyzing the most common factors presented in the literature. I then argue that institutions must consider the particular needs of their senior faculty members and be willing to make change(s) to retain them. In addition, I find that further research can better inform institutions as they diagnose and attend to their senior faculty.

Administration

Although the role of administrative leaders varies from school to school, researchers find that senior faculty members are generally displeased with administrative leadership and less satisfied with their job as a result. In fact, many refer to uncommunicative, incompetent administrative leaders as the cause of their dissatisfaction (Johnsrud and Rosser 2002; Shuster and Finkelstein, 2006). Shuster and Finkelstein (2006) also found that "women and non-Asian minorities are significantly more satisfied with administrative

NEW DIRECTIONS FOR HIGHER EDUCATION, no. 151, Fall 2010 © Wiley Periodicals, Inc.
Published online in Wiley Online Library (wileyonlinelibrary.com) • DOI: 10.1002/he.401

leadership than males and white faculty," and that "junior faculty are more satisfied than senior faculty" (p. 144). The authors also argue that the dissatisfaction of senior faculty members has disproportionately grown at less elite universities because these institutions have become more administratively "micro-managed" over time.

Other researchers suggest that an increasing amount of mundane, bureaucratic work has caused senior faculty members to become dissatisfied. After conducting a study of senior faculty members in the workplace, Clark, Corcoran, and Lewis (1986) found that "the major source of dissatisfaction was the time required for routine bureaucratic tasks (e.g., paperwork) and committees" (p. 185). This suggests that tenured faculty members feel that they have less time for intellectual engagement because they are inundated with administrative duties. And unlike the complaints about administrative incompetence, the dissatisfaction associated with the time required for administrative tasks exists at all levels of higher education (Baldwin, 1990).

Senior faculty members also become dissatisfied with their job when they feel that administrative leaders do not appreciate their work. Institutions with healthy administrator-faculty relations are far more likely to retain their senior faculty. In addition, when senior faculty members feel that administrators genuinely care about their work, they tend to think positively about their role in the organization, and as a result are more attached to the institution (Rousseau, 1995; Baldwin, 1990).

Resources and Support

When the support and appreciation of administrators is coupled with access to sufficient resources, senior faculty members tend to be more satisfied with their jobs. These resources can include graduate assistants, clerical support, assistance with new technology, or parking privileges (Johnsrud and Rosser, 2002). However, senior faculty members strongly value equity in the workplace, and when institutions allocate resources in a manner perceived to be inequitable, senior faculty members who receive less than their colleagues feel undervalued. In fact, senior faculty members often look beyond their own fair treatment and become less satisfied with their job when they believe that their colleagues are being treated unfairly (Gappa, Austin, and Trice, 2007). Clark, Corcoran, and Lewis (1986) support this finding but also emphasize the importance of offering resources that are tied to both teaching and research. When an institution offers adequate resources in one of these areas but not in the other, senior faculty members tend to be less engaged. Bataille and Brown (2006) suggest that senior faculty members are particularly sensitive to the equitable allocation of resources because they often explore new research paths late in their career and seek access to key resources to jump-start their work. When these resources are unavailable or inadequate, senior faculty members, especially in the sciences, are more likely to change jobs (Ehrenberg, Rizzo, and Jakubson, 2003).

Senior faculty members also seek adequate support from their professorial and administrative peers when using an institution's resources. Ambrose, Huston, and Norman (2005) suggest that 40 percent of senior faculty members feel unsupported by their academic and administrative colleagues at the implementation stage. Instructional technology is a good example; many senior faculty members have attempted to use instructional technology only to become frustrated and dissatisfied with the training and support they received (Shuster and Finkelstein, 2006). Although the availability of resources is critical, it is not sufficient; senior faculty members require the proper assistance and support to use these resources effectively and efficiently (Gappa, Austin, and Trice, 2007).

Culture and Collegiality

Ambrose, Huston and Norman (2005) say that collegiality is the one issue that senior faculty members cite most frequently when discussing their job satisfaction. Specifically, cultures that foster collegial relationships tend to have better success at retaining senior faculty members than those that are more fractionalized. And, senior faculty members with strong collegial relationships tend to be more productive. Having supportive relationships allows senior faculty members to focus on their work and to worry less about "backstabbing" and internal competition (Johnsrud and Rosser, 2002; Woods and others, 1997).

Some authors also highlight the importance of collegial relationships within departments as a key component in the job satisfaction of senior faculty members. Senior faculty members are more likely to leave their institution when they experience intra-departmental competition over scarce resources such as research funding, graduate students, and laboratory space. In such departments, secrecy and cliques can develop, causing discomfort and distraction for many senior faculty members (Ambrose, Huston, and Norman, 2005). In addition, senior faculty members tend to be dissatisfied when intellectual ideas are not respected or exchanged freely, which often happens when there is conflict between emerging and more traditional disciplines (Norman, Ambrose, and Huston, 2006).

Salary and Benefits

Although senior faculty members seek a culture of collegiality and fairness, they also desire a competitive pay structure based on performance. However, the percentage of faculty that consider their salary to be too low has risen over the last 40 years, and this rise has been commensurate with the growth in senior faculty members reporting that they are dissatisfied with their job. Considering this pattern, many have argued that senior faculty members are more likely to stay at their current institution if their pay is competitive relative to peer institutions (Bataille and Brown, 2006; Shuster and Finkelstein, 2006). Others add that competitive salaries can motivate senior faculty members to perform at higher levels (Gappa, Austin, and Trice, 2007; Johnsrud and Rosser, 2002). Fairweather (1996) concurs with this point and suggests that administrators can strongly influence the behavior of senior faculty members by developing pay incentives associated with teaching and research. Senior faculty members who receive pay raises in recognition of their work are less likely to doubt the value of their accomplishments and their institution's appreciation (Gappa, Austin, and Trice, 2007).

Other researchers argue that benefits must be considered in conjunction with salary when discussing the job satisfaction of senior faculty members. The rising costs of health care and fuel have caused many senior faculty members to reconsider leaving their institution because of the economic stability provided by their benefits. Thus, administrative adjustments to benefit packages can significantly affect a senior faculty member's satisfaction with their institution. When benefits are cut back, senior faculty members often consider leaving for more generous health insurance and retirement perks at peer institutions (Bataille and Brown, 2006).

Some authors argue that salary and benefits play a less significant role in the satisfaction of senior faculty members when compared with other factors like collegiality and departmental leadership. Ambrose, Huston, and Norman (2005) say that the salary of senior faculty members "generally acts as a catalyst in decisions to leave when compounded by other, more powerful sources of dissatisfaction" (p. 813). Administrators commonly place too much importance on salary when trying to retain senior faculty members and neglect more important factors such as limited resources, administrative interference, and a non-collegial environment. Blackburn and Lawrence (1995) argue that there is not enough evidence to prove that salary and benefits are significant factors in retaining senior faculty members. Although there is a correlation between a senior faculty member's salary and the number of his or her publications, there is no evidence to prove that salary causes faculty to stay at or leave their institution.

Autonomy and the Pursuit of Knowledge

Although senior faculty members desire rewards and recognition for their hard work, they also stress the importance of autonomy. Gappa, Austin, and Trice (2007) argue that "faculty members choose an academic career because it offers autonomy, intellectual challenges, and freedom to pursue personal interests" (p. 105). Although motivated by intellectual stimulation and independence, senior faculty members also want their work to contribute to the mission of their institution and to leave a lasting legacy that validates their importance. A recent survey of senior faculty members indicated that "98 percent rated intellectual stimulation and 94 percent rated contributions to their institution as key sources of satisfaction" (Bataille and Brown, 2006, p. 114). This survey also indicated that a top reason for senior faculty members to leave an institution or to retire was that they were no longer performing up to their own expectations (Bataille and Brown, 2006).

Studies also suggest that senior faculty members are more satisfied when they are engaged in research as opposed to teaching. As a result, Shuster and Finkelstein (2006) argue that senior faculty members at large research universities and elite liberal arts colleges with relatively limited teaching requirements are more likely to be satisfied with their work and to stay at their institution. Furthermore, senior faculty members are more energized by collaborative, interdisciplinary research projects because they provide an added intellectual challenge. Such projects can provide senior faculty members with a sense of professional renewal (Baldwin, 1990). And, when senior faculty members work at an institution that supports interdisciplinary research, they feel more satisfied and are more likely to stay in their current role (Ambrose, Huston, and Norman, 2005).

Many senior faculty members also emphasize the pace and direction of their work as a critical source of satisfaction. They like to feel that they are their own boss and that they determine the design and tempo of their research (Baldwin and Blackburn, 1981; Bess, 1998). In addition, senior faculty members tend to seek variety and change by investigating new fields and by testing new research methods (Baldwin and Blackburn, 1981; Clark, Corcoran, and Lewis, 1986). They are more likely to stay at their current institution if they have the freedom and the opportunity to grow both inside and outside their field of expertise (Baldwin and Blackburn, 1981).

Workload

Some authors argue that while autonomy is important, its true value is only realized when senior faculty members are given ample time to pursue their intellectual interests (Johnsrud and Rosser, 2002; Turner and Boice, 1987). However, the length of the faculty workweek has increased over the last few decades, causing dissatisfaction among faculty members. Researchers have found that "when faculty members experience frustration due to time constraints, they are significantly more likely to report that they intend to leave academia" (Gappa, Austin, and Trice, 2007, p. 116). In fact, survey data indicates that 31 percent of senior faculty members are considering work outside of the academy. For many senior faculty members, especially in professional fields like law and business, a lower time commitment and higher salary in the corporate sector is increasingly attractive (Gappa, Austin, and Trice, 2007).

Many authors also suggest that the root of workload dissatisfaction can be attributed to a scholarly culture that rewards groundbreaking research and publication in top-tier journals. Achieving these goals can require a significant investment of time and result in considerable stress on a faculty member's professional and personal life (Shuster and Finkelstein, 2006). Bataille and Brown (2006) say that it is for these reasons that many senior faculty members decide to leave an institution or to retire. In a survey of senior faculty members, Bataille and Brown found that a primary reason for early retirement was that they were "feeling burned out" (p. 115). Because academe tends to value the individual contribution, especially when considering research publications, the pressure on senior faculty members to achieve greatness can be burdensome and draining. Interestingly, Baldwin (1990) found that senior faculty members with manageable short-term goals were far more likely to be satisfied with their job than those with multiple long-term goals. This finding suggests that when senior faculty members manage their workload in small increments, they are more likely to be satisfied with their job.

Conclusions and Recommendations

A review of the literature surrounding the workplace satisfaction of senior faculty members reveals that it is important that college and university leaders strike a balance with their senior faculty with regard to administrative affairs. Although senior faculty members prefer to be involved in some administrative decisions, there are others of less importance that can inundate and frustrate them. Communication between senior faculty members and administrators is critical for the right balance to be reached. Administrators will have a difficult time collaborating with senior faculty members without knowing the issues that matter to them most. Furthermore, administrators must show appreciation for the academic and administrative work done by senior faculty members. This must be a two-way street, however, because administrators should also feel appreciated when working with senior faculty members. And, if communication and appreciation are not commonly practiced at an institution, it may require making cultural adjustments. Changing an institution's culture is not an easy task, but if institutions hope to attract and retain senior faculty members, it may be necessary (Deal, 1985).

Administrators can also influence the workplace satisfaction of senior faculty members by providing adequate and equitable access to key resources. Because senior faculty members often take their research in new directions, they are particularly sensitive to resource allocation and inequitable distribution. However, providing these resources in an equitable manner is not sufficient. As colleges and universities increasingly adopt new technological innovations, it is critical that administrators provide ample training and technical support for the senior faculty members that use them. In addition, it is important that resources and support be provided for both teaching and research. Senior faculty members that receive one and not the other are more likely to become dissatisfied and to consider leaving their institution.

Equitable resource allocation and supportive peers are characteristics of another important theme cited by researchers: collegial work environments. Senior faculty members tend to be more satisfied and more productive when

NEW DIRECTIONS FOR HIGHER EDUCATION • DOI: 10.1002/he

there is a sense of community at their institution. As a result, institutions should foster an environment that is supportive and that encourages healthy competition. A particular emphasis should be placed within academic departments where senior faculty members are most sensitive to collegiality. Encouraging faculty to engage in collaborative, intra-departmental research and teaching projects, especially when combining new and traditional fields, could create more collegial relationships and more satisfied senior faculty members. However, because such collaborative efforts could be difficult to cultivate, it is imperative that the proposed collaborations come from within the faculty. If administrators promote such activities, they are likely to be seen as meddling in academic affairs or even as violating academic freedom.

Another recurring issue in the literature is the role that salary and benefits play in the job satisfaction of senior faculty members. Some authors argue that salary is a strong motivator for senior faculty members and that institutions must pay competitive wages to retain them. Others claim that benefits are equally as important because senior faculty members feel that they provide stability in tumultuous economic circumstances. Still others say that salary and benefits play a small role in the satisfaction of senior faculty members and that other factors such as collegiality and resources have a larger impact. Considering these perspectives, colleges and universities should offer salaries to senior faculty members that are competitive in relation to peer institutions. However, a narrow focus on competitive salaries can be damaging if other factors such as benefits, collegiality, and research support are neglected. And, cutting or trimming work benefits should be avoided, especially in a tough economy, because senior faculty members are particularly sensitive to such changes.

Another common theme in the literature is the importance of autonomy. Many senior faculty members want to contribute to their institution's mission and to leave a legacy. In doing so, researchers say that these faculty members would rather conduct interdisciplinary research as opposed to teaching. This type of work provides them with fresh intellectual challenges as well as professional renewal. Therefore, if institutions are to retain their senior faculty members they must refrain from interfering and allow them to set the pace and agenda of their work. In addition, they should help foster collaborative research partnerships that cross disciplinary lines when possible. Such opportunities can stimulate senior faculty members and allow them to expand their expertise. It is also important for institutions to gauge the individual preferences of senior faculty members with regard to teaching and research. Though balancing these individual preferences can be difficult, it can help to prevent senior faculty dissatisfaction.

Research also suggests that an increasing workload has caused many senior faculty members to feel overwhelmed and dissatisfied with their work. The average workweek of senior faculty members has lengthened over time, causing almost a third to consider higher wages and fewer hours in occupations outside of the academy. Some authors point to the pressure to produce groundbreaking research as the main force behind senior faculty member burnout. In general, there is agreement that time is a senior faculty member's scarcest resource and that workload issues are pervasive across higher education. Baldwin (1990) suggests that faculty chairs and mentors can help senior faculty members feel less overwhelmed and more satisfied with their work by advising them to set manageable, short-term goals. Although the value placed on research publications and awards is an integral part of the academy's culture, institutions must do a better job of managing the pressure and workload of senior faculty members.

The current literature provides a valuable analysis of senior faculty member satisfaction that can inform institutional decision making. There are, however, areas where further research would provide a deeper understanding of this particular demographic. For example, it may be valuable to research how senior faculty member job satisfaction differs across academic disciplines because each has its own particular subculture. This information could allow institutional leaders to make more effective, customized decisions. Similarly, further research that looks at senior faculty member job satisfaction across institution type may also be valuable. The factors that cause a senior faculty member to leave a public research university may be completely different from those at a private liberal arts college. These factors may also vary by selectivity, institutional resources, or whether the institution is non-profit or for-profit. Finally, though there is some data on senior faculty member job satisfaction by gender and race, further research in this area would provide critical information for institutions trying to recruit and retain a diverse faculty.

Due to the declining job satisfaction of senior faculty members, researchers have examined the factors that influence a faculty member's decision to stay at or to leave their institution. The resulting literature discusses many variables that affect a senior faculty member's career, including administrative affairs, resource allocation, and the importance of fostering a collegial environment. It also examines the effects of salary and benefits, the value placed on autonomy, and the increasing workload of senior faculty members. The literature also reveals a need for further research that looks at senior faculty member job satisfaction by academic discipline, institutional type, gender, and race. Filling these research gaps can help institutions make informed decisions that are tailored to their particular situation. As tenured professionals with the potential to make revolutionary discoveries, senior faculty members are one of an institution's most precious resources. If colleges and universities are to reverse the current trend in job dissatisfaction and retain a vital senior faculty, they must address the specific needs of this demographic with both the resources and willingness to make change.

References

Ambrose, S., Huston, T., and Norman, M. "A Qualitative Method for Assessing Faculty Satisfaction." *Research in Higher Education*, 2005, 46(7), 803–830. Retrieved February

3, 2009, from http://web.ebscohost.com.ezp-prod1.hul.harvard.edu/ehost/pdfviewer/pdfviewer?vid=2&hid=7&sid=d9dc1a38–5b1a-4330-a055–4033dbd5425f%40sessionmgr10

Baldwin, R. "Faculty Vitality beyond the Research University: Extending a Contextual Concept." *Journal of Higher Education (Columbus, Ohio)*, 1990, *61*, 160–180. Retrieved February 3, 2009, from http://www.jstor.org/stable/1981960

Baldwin, R. G., and Blackburn, R. T. "The Academic Career as a Developmental Process: Implications for Higher Education." *Journal of Higher Education*, 1981, *52*, 598–614.

Bataille, G., and Brown, B. "Faculty Career Paths: Multiple Routes to Academic Success and Satisfaction." Westport, Conn.: Praeger Publishers, 2006.

Bess, J. "Contract Systems, Bureaucracies, and Faculty Motivation." *Journal of Higher Education*, 1998, *69*(1), 1–22. Retrieved February 9, 2009, from http://www.jstor.org/pss/2649180

Blackburn, R., and Lawrence, J. *Faculty at Work: Motivation, Expectation, Satisfaction.* Baltimore, Md.: The Johns Hopkins University Press, 1995.

Clark, S., Corcoran, M., and Lewis, D. "The Case for an Institutional Perspective on Faculty Development." *Journal of Higher Education (Columbus, Ohio)*, 1986, *57*, 176–195. Retrieved March 17, 2009, from http://www.jstor.org/pss/1981480

Deal, T. "Cultural Change: Opportunity, Silent Killer; or Metamorphosis?" In R. Kilmann, M. Saxton, and R. Serpa (eds.), *Gaining Control of the Corporate Culture.* San Francisco: Jossey-Bass, 1985.

Ehrenberg, R. G., Rizzo, M. R., and Jakubson, G. H. "Who Bears the Growing Cost of Science at Universities?" (Cornell Higher Education Research Institute, Working Paper 35). Ithaca, N.Y.: Cornell University, 2003.

Fairweather, J. *Faculty Work and Public Trust: Restoring the Value of Teaching and Public Service in American Academic Life.* Needham Heights, Mass.: Allyn and Bacon, 1996.

Farrell, D. "Exit, Voice, Loyalty and Neglect as Responses to Job Dissatisfaction: A Multidimensional Scaling Study." *Academy of Management Journal*, 1983, *26*, 596–607.

Gappa, J., Austin, A., and Trice, A. *Rethinking Faculty Work: Higher Education's Strategic Imperative.* San Francisco: Jossey-Bass, 2007.

Huston, T., Norman, M., and Ambrose, S. "Expanding the Discussion of Faculty Vitality to Include Productive but Disengaged Senior Faculty." *Journal of Higher Education*, 2007, *78*(5), 493–522. Retrieved April 14, 2009, from http://web.ebscohost.com.ezp-prod1.hul.harvard.edu/ehost/pdfviewer/pdfviewer?vid=12&hid=7&sid=061b7728–76ce-429f-847d-420c71963632%40sessionmgr12

Johnsrud, L. K., and Rosser, V. J. "Faculty Members' Morale and Their Intention to Leave." *The Journal of Higher Education*, 2002, *73*, 518–541.

Norman, M., Ambrose, S., and Huston, T. "Assessing and Addressing Faculty Morale: Cultivating Consciousness, Empathy, and Empowerment." *Review of Higher Education*, 2006, *29*(3), 347–379. Retrieved April 6, 2009, from http://muse.jhu.edu.ezp-prod1.hul.harvard.edu/journals/review_of_higher_education/v029/29.3norman.html

Rousseau, D. M. *Psychological Contracts in Organizations: Understanding Written and Unwritten Agreements.* Thousand Oaks, Calif.: Sage, 1995.

Shuster, J., and Finkelstein, M. *The American Faculty: The Restructuring of Academic Work and Careers.* Baltimore, Md.: The Johns Hopkins University Press, 2006.

Turner, J. L., and Boice, R. "Starting at the Beginning: The Concerns and Needs of New Faculty." In J. Kurfiss, L. Hilsen, L. Mortensen, and R. Wadworth (eds.), *To Improve the Academy: Vol. 6. Resources for Faculty, Instructional, and Organizational Development.* Stillwater, Okla.: New Forums Press, 1987.

U.S. Department of Education. "National Center for Education Statistics, Digest of Education Statistics: 2008." Washington, D.C.: U.S. Department of Education, 2007.

Retrieved February 24, 2010, from http://nces.ed.gov/programs/digest/d08/tables/dt08_249.asp?referrer=list

Woods, S. E., Reid, A., Arndt, J. E., Curtis, P., and Stritter, F. T. "Collegial Networking and Faculty Vitality." *Family Medicine*, 1997, *29*(1), 45–49.

BRENDAN C. RUSSELL is a doctoral candidate at the Harvard Graduate School of Education and Research Assistant, the Collaborative on Academic Careers in Higher Education (COACHE).

NEW DIRECTIONS FOR HIGHER EDUCATION • DOI: 10.1002/he

7

Shared governance between administration and faculty needs to be viewed as a sanctioned vehicle of collaboration, not a rivalry.

The Future of Shared Governance

Matthew A. Crellin

Higher education has relied on the power of collaborative decision making on college and university campuses through the model of shared governance since the early 1900s (Tierney and Lechuga, 2004). However, the principles of shared governance are now more thoroughly tested than ever before. In response to these simultaneous pressures and challenges, the leadership of education must be at once both agile and purposeful while drawing upon a deeper well of knowledge to inform its decision making. The current model of governance has notable weaknesses, not the least of which is the tension that exists when constituents come together with competing and, at times, antithetical demands and expectations. Although the issues in academe are changing, the structures have remained relatively static, calling into question both the relevancy of shared governance and its feasibility in modern times.

Analyzing shared governance in this context should not seek to radically suggest changes to the system by rewriting the principles that are steeped in tradition. The presented assumption, however, is that the many changes and challenges that are "at academe's doorstep" (Tierney and Lechuga, 2004) require colleges and universities to rethink shared governance.

Internal and External Stresses on Shared Governance

Since the issuing of the "Joint Statement" from the American Association of University Professors (AAUP), higher education governance has become increasingly complex, especially in light of increased organizational stress (Birnbaum, 1988; Kezar, 2001; Kezar, 2004). The challenges on shared governance range in almost every conceivable direction.

Part of the confusion about shared governance has to do with its quality as, what Gary Olson calls, a "floating signifier"—a term so stripped of

New Directions for Higher Education, no. 151, Fall 2010 © Wiley Periodicals, Inc.
Published online in Wiley Online Library (wileyonlinelibrary.com) • DOI: 10.1002/he.402

any definitive meaning that it becomes molded around the context a particular person or group decides to give it in the current moment (Olson, 2009). Shared governance has certainly established itself as the preeminent intergroup structure in higher education, yet the definitions of authority remain situational at best and vague at worst. Some faculty members believe, as Olson points out, that shared governance imbues faculty to delegate governance of the university to administrators, keeping academics at the heart of the university while administrators are left to perform the "more distasteful managerial labor" (Olson, 2009). Trustees and administration may view shared governance in the opposite manner, choosing to view faculty as important contributors to the conversation, but nevertheless believing that administrative decisions should be the purview of the administration. Even if shared governance presupposed that all parties have an equal say, are some, in the words of George Orwell, "more equal than others"? Reflecting on leadership within the university, I am reminded of the historical theories of the universe: At one time, scholars argued the models of the geocentric and heliocentric universe—the celestial bodies revolved in space, but around what they revolved remained a debate. Although the Copernican heliocentric model replaced the Ptolemaic model of the early modern age, the authority seat of the academy may prove harder to define—although one in five Americans may still believe that the sun revolves around the earth (Dean, 2005).

The sustainability of shared governance rests on several actionable items: the academy's ability to meet escalating external changes, a re-endowment of the definitions of governance through a shared taxonomy, and an introduction of new principles of intergroup leadership.

Changing Realities that Re-prioritize Governance

Is shared governance ill-equipped to meet the needs of modern times? Peter Eckel and Adrianna Kezar list four changes with the potential to reshape academic decision making. The first is the relationship that state governments have with public institutions, most notably the increased scrutiny and accountability measures that lawmakers are demanding with regard to student learning and levels of research (Eckel and Kezar, 2006).

Second, the decline in public support means that institutions must look toward other revenue-generating activities to ensure a return on investment (Bok, 2003), including increases in technology, sponsored research, intellectual property claims, market influences, and the adaptation toward business-based decision-making skills (American Federation of Teachers, 2008).

Third, globalization requires a new style of leadership as the addition of international components, global partnerships, delivery of joint programs, and international dimensions not only add more stakeholders to the leadership roundtable, but force universities to interact with new competitors and markets (Eckel and Kezar, 2006).

NEW DIRECTIONS FOR HIGHER EDUCATION • DOI: 10.1002/he

Fourth, the changing academic workforce has significant implications for governance. The number of full-time faculty continues to decline while the use of adjuncts is on the rise: in the 1970s, 80 percent of faculty were full-time, tenure track professors and in 2000 numbered only 50 percent; in Massachusetts community colleges, for example, up to 80 percent of faculty are part-time (Eckel and Kezar, 2006; Kezar, 2001; McLaughlin, 2009).

According to Dr. Larry Gerber, Chair of the AAUP's Committee on College and University Governance (personal e-mail communication, December 4, 2009), this change in faculty may add greater stress to the system:

> The biggest problem here (in shared governance) is in the growth of contingent, non-tenure track faculty. The growth in the number of faculty falling into this category has the effect of undermining shared governance and academic freedom. It is necessary to find appropriate means to involve contingent faculty in governance, but this raises difficult issues, both because these faculty are more subject to pressure from administrators than tenured faculty, and also because tenured faculty are more reluctant to cede some authority to those who may not have a long-term commitment to the institution.

Criticisms to the Calls for Revision and Examining the Tenability of Shared Governance

Although some criticize shared governance as no longer relevant, others note that many higher education institutions have responded successfully to market and external pressures: integrating new technologies; "establishing joint programs with industry, offering external degrees"; and retooling academic disciplines to better meet the demands of employers (Birnbaum, 2004). In fact, some aspects of shared governance may be beneficial. When I asked AAUP Governance Chair Larry Gerber about the criticisms of shared governance, he cited a need for both faculty senates and administrators to seek improvements on intergroup collaboration (personal communication, December 4, 2009):

> One of the most common criticisms of the shared governance model is that faculty bodies take too long to make decisions. I think that there is some validity to this, but it is also the case that curricula should not be changing every year to keep up with the latest fads. Higher education should not be trying to constantly "market" new products in response to transitory "customer" demands. On the other hand, the functioning of faculty senates can be improved by building in set time frames for decision making. It may also be necessary to devise better means allowing for inter-departmental cooperation, so that departmental and college structures do not become obstacles to needed change.

According to Professor Gerber, the strength of shared governance lies in its ability to act as a guideline for which governance and collaboration can be enhanced: "the AAUP's 1966 statement on government still sets forth sound principles as to the distribution of authority. It offers only very general guidelines, not prescriptions about how exactly governance ought to be structured, but properly argues that faculty should have primary responsibility for academic matters, since they have the greatest expertise." Such a model does not portray the governance of higher education as a hierarchy; rather, the model allows for the two-way flow of decision making to come from the board of trustees or regents through the administration in conjunction with the faculty (AAUP, 2003).

Examples of Shared Governance in the Global Age: Online Learning at Southern New Hampshire University

In recent years, higher education has expanded into new areas (e.g., for-profit instruction, distance education, new research alliances, and the development of technology and courseware) that Mallon (2005) calls the "suburbs of the university." These expanded areas have the potential to bring about new models of decision making and call into question whether or not shared governance is appropriate to apply across these news arms of the university.

At Southern New Hampshire University, the College of Online and Continuing Education (COCE) is a highly successful and relatively new division responsible for "extending SNHU's offerings to part-time students and/or those not enrolled at the main campus" (P. LeBlanc, personal e-mail communication, November 20, 2009). The online program was recently selected for the second time as a winner in the *New Hampshire Business Review's* "Best of Business" in the Best Online Degree Programs category along with the campus-based School of Business for its "Best M.B.A. Degree," which earned its award for the third time (P. LeBlanc, personal e-mail communication, November 20, 2009). The online program is a revenue-generating entity for the university, accounting for its entire annual surplus and has attracted both accolades and increased enrollment for SNHU (P. LeBlanc, personal e-mail communication, March 8, 2010).

With the COCE came new challenges: the COCE was principally overseen by a management team and chiefly taught by part-time, adjunct faculty members. One goal of the COCE program was to offer the same breadth of courses and topics online as the traditional campus or university college (UC). As the COCE gained institutional traction, faculty from the UC began to raise questions about the content of the online program, the manner in which their course materials were being delivered, and the procedures for managing the program. Dr. Susan Schragle-Law, Professor of Organizational Leadership and President of the Faculty Senate at SNHU (personal communication, December 2, 2009), explained that the online program went through several iterations that eventually took it further away from shared governance, and made it a matter of increasing concern of faculty members:

> The issues surrounding the online college (COCE) are still an ongoing conversation among the faculty. A decade ago, some faculty were resistant to accepting online delivery of their programs: That principled resistance no longer exists. However, the faculty has remained divided on the processes used to port their courses into the online division. In some situations. . .some faculty are accepting while others are not. Some faculty members remain uncomfortable about their say in the online division. The president (SNHU President Paul Leblanc) has made it clear that online is a revenue-generating area that is here to stay. Online went through a few changes years ago, including a new director of the COCE who really became distant from the faculty. [President LeBlanc] said that the COCE pulled out of traditional governance in order to establish programs and grow and develop.

Analyses of these issues reveal the classic tension that can exist in shared governance. Administrators felt that the methods to deliver this new content often looked to traditional faculty governance as a source of slowness regarding the push of content through the COCE (P. LeBlanc, personal communication, March 8, 2010). The director and administrators within the COCE imported and emphasized business-like agility in the extended delivery process, which Dr. Schragle-Law said, "seemed to put up roadblocks to restrict any full-time faculty input into the academic quality and content of online courses" (personal e-mail communication, March 12, 2010). Meanwhile, some faculty members argued that the quality of the curriculum was best preserved by faculty oversight.

To solve this issue, President LeBlanc and Vice President for Academic Affairs Patricia Lynott proposed a new approval procedure for the COCE. A program that exists in the UC could move to the COCE for extended delivery after going through seven steps to port the material for distribution to online students, including a thorough review from UC stakeholders and professors, curriculum committee review within the COCE, and a multitiered decision tree allowing for the multidirectional flow of ideas and suggestions to pass through both entities to address their concerns and refine changes to coursework. COCE additionally has the license to develop programs that do not exist in the UC catalog as well (P. LeBlanc, personal e-mail communication, March 8, 2010).

Quality control, a concern of faculty members like Professor Schragle-Law, is now addressed by incorporating faculty to have input in the core items of the course content. Full-time professors are invited to participate as course reviewers to review the completed work of the course authors (adjunct teachers) and provide feedback and suggestions, allowing faculty at the UC to flag critical omissions and review of "content enhanced courses," which are purely developed for online delivery. Lastly, course quality is monitored through course author performance. Mechanisms for quality oversight

NEW DIRECTIONS FOR HIGHER EDUCATION • DOI: 10.1002/he

include performance reviews, pedagogy training, syllabus review, online activity reporting, and an online grievance process that allows complaints to move through a four-stage administrative review process.

Analysis of the Governance Structure in the College of Online and Continuing Education

President LeBlanc wanted to move the COCE in a new direction. To accomplish this, he needed the COCE to compete with other online education providers. According to LeBlanc, faculty approval proved necessary to ensure the quality and legitimacy of the program. LeBlanc stressed the need to "pull our non-traditional programs further out of the traditional campus governance model," adding that "it took a long time to get faculty buy-in and some still think they are giving up too much control, but we had to keep the non-traditional—especially online—much more agile than traditional governance allowed" (personal communication, November 20, 2009).

Still, other members of the SNHU faculty remain skeptical about how the online model fits into the role of shared governance. Professor Schragle-Law summarized the sentiments of some faculty members regarding the COCE's governance structure (personal communication, March 12, 2010):

> What's happened here is that we've realized as a faculty that online is here to stay and we're trying to support it by and large and to develop a working relationship with them (the COCE). What is still not clear is how *they* will fit into *our* governance structure. We have governance concerning promotion, governance about sabbaticals, and governance over curriculum development, etc. In the proposal for shared governance over COCE, we are theoretically able to review the curriculum, but only to offer commentary or feedback which can be completely dismissed. We can make suggestions, but they may or may not implement them. President LeBlanc would like to see more collaborative decision making and we're trying to meet this challenge. Still, there's tension between faculty and online administration. We have a lot of adjunct faculty that teach in the UC and COCE. In the mind of many faculty, sometimes we seem to revert back to the days of closed doors and following a chain of command which is not collaborative.

The Culture, Symbolism, and Analysis of Shared Governance in Changing Times

Shared governance is integral to the culture of the academy. It is part tradition, part tactic, and largely symbolic. A recurring theme emerges both in the SNHU example and in the arguments both for and against governance: All parties are increasingly concerned with impact, feelings, and representation both in a real sense but also on levels of trust, meaningful participation, and respect for their expertise.

NEW DIRECTIONS FOR HIGHER EDUCATION • DOI: 10.1002/he

The loosely coupled nature of colleges and universities highlights the tensions of decentralized decision making (Eckel and Kezar, 2006). When decisions are not coordinated across different units, decentralized decision making may place groups at odds. Loosely coupled systems are not without their benefits: They are able to respond to changes with greater flexibility and enable professionals with focused expertise to weigh in on issues and problems without requiring centralized knowledge on all disciplines (Weick, 1979; Eckel & Kezar, 2006). The loosely coupled system, however, may embrace autonomy at the expense of widening the divide among other departments or units within the university.

Competing values, disparate perspectives, and contextual directives often find common ground in educational mission. In the SNHU example, the university was able to push a finished product through the COCE. The faculty involvement and consequent discussion over governance served more of a dialectic purpose than as an exercise in futility. This example does underscore what previous thinkers on shared governance have alluded to: The model values both decisions and the roles of the respective decision-makers. In a symbolic framework, the decisions that may be reached are not as important as what the process of decision making means to the participants involved (Bolman and Deal, 2008).

Continued Analysis: Intergroup Relationship and Navigating Change

A central method to improving the model of shared governance may be found in promoting understanding and fostering deeper, more systemic cooperation between faculty and administrators. Communication is an essential component of the governance process (Tierney and Minor, 2004).

Todd Pittinsky (2009) illustrates the classic tensions that one could easily find in shared governance:

> Any school administrator can tell you that the student body is not only a collection of individual students but also a collection of groups—cliques, teams, ethnic groups, boys and girls, and sometimes gangs—and that these groups matter. Leadership scholars are often concerned with how leaders can define and sustain a collective, without which there would be nothing to lead. But by and large, these scholars have conceptualized this task as the challenge of bringing together individuals, with little thought given to the various subgroups to which those individuals belong. . .(i)ntergroup leadership is defined as leadership that brings groups together. (p. xix)

Researchers have identified a generic tension between groups of internal cohesion—how much group members feel bound together—and external pressure (Pittinsky, 2009, *forthcoming*). Said differently, the stronger that a group feels its own unique collective identity, the more pronounced difference it sees in everyone else, making it easier to wind up in competition or conflict with "the other group." Pittinsky suggests that intergroup leadership requires leaders to mitigate this tension by simultaneously decreasing the bad feelings between groups while creating positive feelings—two separate tasks. This concept, which he has termed "allophilia," focuses on accentuating the factors that groups have in common with one another. Applying this concept to the tensions found in shared governance, it is not enough to bring everyone together to the same table; rather, leaders should work to honor this difference without trying to eliminate diversity of thought.

Dr. Pittinsky further elaborates on his interpretation of intergroup dynamics as it might apply to shared governance (personal communication, December 2, 2009):

> I do think that some intergroup literature is certainly applicable to this relationship. For example, faculty think of themselves as a group: they say the term "faculty" when they describe themselves, they represent an equivalent position. Administrators also have codified their own sense of "we." Here, they think of themselves as constituents. Of course, if this is a unionized context or not, a state university or private, there are additional, clearly delineated lines. But, when you break down the functions of each group further—campus housing, administrators, a faculty senate—the typology in each starts to become contested with each group. Some things are clearly the domain of one particular group while others are too contested to focus. This is where this idea of a high level of allophilia might come into play—this idea of "positive deviance" where each group is different but ought to be positively engaged with one another.

Pittinsky suggests that institutions ought to look to examples of those in the university who have crossed into a different area of the institution for their anecdotes and reflections. For example, someone who worked in a faculty union and was then sent to management not only would have keen insight on how each group works, but would likely experience a shift of allegiance, values, and group identity. Lastly, Pittinsky emphasizes the role that positive attitudes play in improving the tensions of shared governance: "expectations mask reality and stereotypes often cloud the work that is actually being accomplished. Yet, there are such things as positive stereotypes and should be anchored into a context. Such tensions are less about the world it is and more about what people think it is."

Dr. Roderick Kramer expands on this idea (personal communication, December 8, 2009) concerning the implications of trust, stereotypes, and symbolism in negotiations and group dynamics. Kramer offers suggestions of how trust in negotiations and the promotion of positive stereotypes might serve to ease the tensions that so often typify the behavior found in the shared governance model:

> Trust is interesting because working across boundaries so often builds cognitive difference. Groups have different vocabularies and such little face to

face contact that stereotypes emerge about what the other is like—often creating suspicion if not paranoia. Leaders should explore the notion of the "contact hypothesis," which has much to do with facilitating cooperation and structuring systems to create equal status. For example, if I wanted to bridge the difference between the education and business schools at Harvard (as loosely coupled systems) I can presuppose that one certainly has stereotypes about what the other is like . . . working together on things such as a joint seminar or colloquium or panel promotes joint interdependence. While one group may have a pool of greater knowledge than the other, a greater norm begins to shift where people begin to meet on the same plane.

In this aspect, Kramer illustrates an interesting point: too often, groups come together to act on problems rather than to seek points of collaboration that might strengthen their interdependence. Furthermore, if leaders within these groups extend themselves to the other group in a true spirit of openness and respect for the other group's work, this model behavior might serve to reinforce positive behaviors.

Heifetz (2009) suggests that the overriding reason for failure to adapt to change is a resistance and fear of loss:

> Losses come in many forms among individuals, organizations, and societies, from direct losses of goods such as wealth, status, authority, influence, security, and health, to indirect losses such as competence and loyal affiliation. In our experience, the common aphorism that people resist change is more wrong than right. People do not resist change per se; they resist loss. People usually embrace change when they anticipate a clear benefit. Rarely does anyone return a winning lottery ticket. People resist change when change involves the possibility of giving up something they hold dear. (p. 131)

Heifetz identifies two common patterns for "adaptive failure:" diversion of attention and displacement of responsibility. "These take a wide variety of forms in organizations and politics, including using decoys and distracting issues, tackling only the aspects of the problem that fit a group's competence, jumping to solutions without adequate diagnosis, misusing consultants, blaming authority, scapegoating, personalizing the issues, launching ad hominem attacks, and externalizing the enemy" (Heifetz, 2009). Shared governance without principled leadership can quickly devolve into a political exclusion exercise, and leaders should therefore be mindful of the strategies of incorporation and inclusion.

Heifetz's challenge to leadership applies to governance in the university—it requires those who govern to assess "who should play a part in the deliberations and in what sequence?" (p. 133). Kramer provides an interesting suggestion to changing the model of shared governance: "Cognitive thinking is all about the framing of the task. Maybe instead of shared governance, it ought to be called *distributive leadership*. It has a nicer sound in that it's about sharing leadership opportunities across the spectrum. It redistributes the leadership challenges in a way where groups may have more of an equality in answering the challenges of governance by assigning the leadership with intent" (R. Kramer, personal communication. December 8, 2009).

However, would "distributive leadership" just become another floating signifier? Professor Kramer is provocative:

> Giving something like shared governance a new working title in distributive leadership gets people thinking differently about the attribute and domains. For example, we have resources but we're trying to come up with the best way to meet the imperatives and demands on those resources. People out in the collective might have great ideas and distributive leadership might imply that voices have more of a distributed and equal weight. The point here is getting people on the same webpage—on content, on curriculum, on budgets—with the intent to move beyond just getting everyone in the same room. (R. Kramer, personal communication. December 8, 2009)

Re-endowing Shared Governance while Preserving Collegiality

Shared governance is both a means to an end and an end to be maintained and valued; it is a collaborative process while also an outcome of collegiality; it is steeped in tradition yet concerns itself with change and innovation in the academy, and most of all, it seeks to bridge difference and yet curiously exacerbates it. This model is likely not going to be changed radically; there are aspects of this governance structure that work well and promote positive outcomes. There are many ways to proceed, and those in leadership should work to re-endow the term "shared governance" with new meaning and definition to actively prepare higher education to navigate the challenges yet to come.

References

American Association of University Professors (AAUP). "Statement on Government of Colleges and Universities (1967)." Washington, D.C.: American Association of University Professors, 2001.

American Federation of Teachers. "Shared Governance in Colleges and Universities" (Adobe Digital Edition). Washington, D.C.: American Federation of Teachers, 2008. Retrieved December 1, 2009, from http://facultysenate.tamu.edu/Quick%20Links/Shared%20Governance%20in%20Colleges%20and%20Universities.pdf

Birnbaum, R. "The End of Shared Governance: Looking Ahead of Looking Back." In W. Tierney and V. M. Lechuga (eds.), *Restructuring Shared Governance in Higher Education*. New Directions for Teaching and Learning, no. 127. San Francisco: Jossey-Bass, 2004.

Bok, D. *Universities in the Marketplace: The Commercialization of Higher Education*. Princeton, N.J.: Princeton University Press, 2003.

Bolman, L., and Deal, T. *Reframing Organizations: Artistry, Choice, and Leadership.* San Francisco: Jossey-Bass, 2008.

Dean, C. "Scientific savvy? in U.S., Not Much." *The New York Times*, August 30, 2005, p. 1. Retrieved November 30, 2009, from http://www.nytimes.com/2005/08/30/science/30profile.html?_r=1&ex=1184990400&en=2fb126c3132f89ae&ei=5070.

Eckel, P., and Kezar, A. "The Challenges Facing Academic Decision Making: Contemporary Issues and Steadfast Structures." In P. Eckel (ed.), *The Shifting Frontiers of Academic Decision Making: Responding to New Priorities, Following New Pathways.* Westport, Conn.: Praeger Publishers, 2006.

Heifetz, R. "Operating across Boundaries: Leading Adaptive Change." In T. Pittinsky (ed.), *Crossing the Divide: Intergroup Leadership in a World of Difference.* Boston: Harvard Business Press, 2009.

Kezar, A. "Seeking a Sense of Balance: Academic Governance in the 21st Century." *Peer Review*, 2001, *3*(3), 4–6.

Kezar, A. "What Is More Important to Effective Governance: Relationships, Trust, and Leadership or Structures and Formal Processes?" In W. Tierney and V. M. Lechuga (eds.), *Restructuring Shared Governance in Higher Education.* New Directions for Teaching and Learning, no. 127. San Francisco: Jossey-Bass, 2004.

Kramer, R. "Trust Building in Intergroup Negotiations." In T. Pittinsky (ed.), *Crossing the Divide: Intergroup Leadership in a World of Difference.* Boston: Harvard Business Press, 2009.

Mallon, W. T. *Characteristics of Research Centers and Institutes at U.S. Medical Schools and Universities.* Washington, D.C.: Association of American Medical Colleges, 2005.

McLaughlin, J. B. Lecture, Harvard Graduate School of Education, 2009.

Olson, G. "Exactly What Is 'Shared Governance'?" *The Chronicle of Higher Education*, July 23, 2009, p. 1. Retrieved November 28, 2009, from http://chronicle.com.ezp-prod1.hul.harvard.edu/article/Exactly-What-Is-Shared-Gov/47065/

Pittinsky, T. L. (Ed.). *Crossing the Divide: Intergroup Leadership in a World of Difference.* Boston: Harvard Business School Press, 2009.

Pittinsky, T. L. "A Two-Dimensional Theory of Intergroup Leadership: The Case of National Diversity." *American Psychologist, forthcoming.*

Tierney, W. G., and Lechuga, V. M. *Restructuring Shared Governance in Higher Education.* New Directions for Teaching and Learning, no. 127. San Francisco: Jossey-Bass, 2004.

Tierney, W. G., and Minor, J. T. "A Cultural Perspective on Communication and Governance." In W. Tierney and V. M. Lechuga (eds.), *Restructuring Shared Governance in Higher Education.* New Directions for Teaching and Learning, no. 127. San Francisco: Jossey-Bass, 2004.

Weick, K. *The Social Psychology of Organizing.* Reading, Mass.: Addison-Wesley, 1979.

MATTHEW A. CRELLIN *is director of Policy and Research at the New England Board of Higher Education.*

8

A decision to close a famous art museum exposes ambiguities in governance and leadership.

The Rose Art Museum Crisis

Paul Dillon

On January 26, 2009, the Brandeis University Board of Trustees voted unanimously to close the Rose Art Museum (Waltham, Mass.). The proceeds from the subsequent auction were to be reinvested in the university to ensure its long-term financial health. The reaction to the decision by campus constituencies provides a case study to show the complex nature of universities as organizations. Universities are not top-down, linear organizations designed to rationally execute a business plan. Instead, they are complex, amorphous, and often convoluted organizations that can simultaneously embrace multiple missions, priorities, and decision-making processes within a single overarching framework.

With complexity comes challenges. It is widely acknowledged that administrative leadership at colleges and universities face constraints when implementing decisions that affect the long-term goals and mission of the university. However, organizational complexity does not alone explain why Brandeis leadership faced such resistance to the decision to close the Rose.

It will be shown that aspects of Brandeis's organizational culture compounded the crisis. Several constituencies reacted in different ways to the decision, exposing a larger dissonance in the perceived mission of the university. Together, organizational culture, constrained leadership, and autonomously acting university constituencies combined, along with the presence of a financial crisis, to temporarily fracture Brandeis's collective sense of purpose and vision for the future.

The Rose Art Museum crisis demonstrates that effective leadership requires not only a rational assessment of a university's financial and resource needs, it also requires a non-rational emotional component, an organizational EQ, that can harness the collective ambitions of different constituencies toward a commonly shared goal. If meaningful and legitimate relationships are not carefully cultivated and maintained through collaboration,

NEW DIRECTIONS FOR HIGHER EDUCATION, no. 151, Fall 2010 © Wiley Periodicals, Inc.
Published online in Wiley Online Library (wileyonlinelibrary.com) • DOI: 10.1002/he.403

coalition-building, and sheer political calculation, then situations like the Rose Art Museum are not only possible, but also likely.

Brandeis University: A Brief Organizational History

Brandeis University was founded in 1948. The goal was to create a nonsectarian university that symbolized the achievements and accomplishments of the Jewish faith. From its inception, Brandeis harbored lofty ambitions. As Brandeis's first president, Abram Sachar, put it, "If they [the Jews] are going to create a symbol, it better be a symbol of excellence. . . We have to have a Harvard/Yale/Princeton/ Columbia/Dartmouth type of school. . . ." (as quoted in Freeland, 1992, p. 188).

As its leader, Sachar set out to legitimize the new university in the eyes of the rest of the academic community. A gifted fundraiser, he helped build the university from the ground up and in the process forged a stellar academic reputation. Scholar Richard Freeland observed that Sachar was extremely proud of Brandeis's accomplishments and often regarded the university as his personal responsibility (Freeland, 2009).

In doing so, Sachar set a leadership tone and style that would perpetuate throughout the school's history. Emphasizing results and accomplishments over participatory governance, Sachar often employed a "divide and conquer" approach to faculty relations, and often acted unilaterally without regard to faculty opinion (G. Fellman, personal communication, November 23, 2009). This precedent occurred during a formative period for the organization. Lacking similar peers, established traditions, and preexisting institutional mythologies, the inter-organizational relationships built in the 1950s and 1960s would solidify into patterns of behavior that would form elements of the university's nascent organizational culture. Ambition and growth, qualities embraced and nurtured by Sachar, would go on to form part of Brandeis's collective identity.

The Rose Art Museum was founded during this period, officially opening its doors on May 3, 1961. Serendipitously, the founding of the Rose Art Museum corresponded with a robust and creative period in the American art world. From 1962 to 1963, while still in its infancy, the Rose Art Museum purchased $50,000 worth of artwork from young and upcoming artists, particularly from the American Abstract Expressionist movement. These purchases, which helped establish the museum, would later appreciate to a value estimated at $200 million (Rush, 2009). Mirroring the growth of its host institution, the Rose would quickly build a reputation as one of the finest collections of contemporary art in the country.

Sachar's departure from the presidency in 1968 represented one of the high-water marks in Brandeis history. Inevitably, however, growth and expansion began to require the less glamorous responsibilities of general maintenance. This transitional period also coincided with the social unrest and student activism of the late 1960s. Organizational tensions between students,

NEW DIRECTIONS FOR HIGHER EDUCATION • DOI: 10.1002/he

staff, and university administration grew during this time. Incidents emerged that began to show the underlying tensions that existed within the organization. In January 1969, disaffected students seized Ford Hall, at the time the headquarters of university administration. The standoff lasted for eleven days. Although it eventually reached a peaceful resolution, it had a dramatic impact on the character of the institution. First, it set an adversarial tone for inter-organizational relations. Second, it caused anxiety among donors and board members concerned about the perceptions of Brandeis within the larger context of society and higher education (Freeland, 2009).

In the 1970s, university growth would continue, but it lost the momentum built during the previous two decades. The university faced the problem of the debts and other financial burdens, including dipping enrollment numbers. Debating the goals and mission of Brandeis University would become a recurring theme as the organization tried to reconcile its ambitious aims with economic realities.

The 1980s can be characterized as a period of modest institutional growth. During this time, however, university constituencies continually struggled to act in concert. One incident in particular highlights these underlying tensions. In 1987, prompted by concerns about financial health of the university, a Board of Trustees committee recommended that the school "tone down" its associations with the Jewish community and culture to make it more attractive to a wider pool of applicants (McLaughlin and Reck, 1997, pp. 2–3). The administration first implemented the policy by quietly offering bacon and other non-kosher food to students during the summer of 1987. Within weeks, a controversy brewed among several university constituents, including the students, faculty, and media (McLaughlin, and Reck, 1997).

In a pattern that would be replicated in the Rose Art Museum incident, the university struggled to articulate a coherent and unified identity and mission as a collective entity. While leadership decisions moved forward with their decision to re-brand the university, many internal constituencies, including faculty, staff, and donors, resisted administration efforts. An article in the *New York Times* summed up the controversy when it suggested that the debate was about the "soul" of Brandeis and the degree to which its Jewish identity was fundamental to the mission of the university (Wald, 1987). Echoes of these very questions would again resurface in the Rose Art Museum crisis of 2009. Instead of debating its Jewish identity, Brandeis would struggle with questions over how much culture, that is, art, remained central to its core mission.

In 1994 President Jehuda Reinharz stepped in to reinvigorate Brandeis University; he was very successful. During the Reinharz tenure, Brandeis tripled its endowment and reaffirmed its commitment to academic excellence (Schworm, 2009). In 1997 the university was recognized as first among eleven "nationally rising" research universities (Brandeis University, n.d.). Throughout Reinharz's tenure, Brandeis remained among the top thirty-five national universities in the *U.S. News and World Report* ranking. In an era of increased competition among schools, Brandeis managed to increase its admissions selectivity, continued an aggressive pace of capital improvements, and expanded its academic offerings. (Shworm, 2009). President Reinharz also took steps to put the university on a firmer financial footing by implementing reforms to bring endowment spending policies in line with industry standards (Brandeis community member, personal communication, December 2, 2009).

Within the campus community, Reinharz earned respect for his contributions to the university's success. However, he also developed a reputation for having a distant and hierarchical management style. Former Student Union President Andrew Hogan expressed to me in an interview that the student body—rightly or wrongly—developed an opinion that the university president was not heavily involved with student affairs and was focused more on fundraising (personal communication, November 17, 2009). Despite the university's success, several minor incidents began to feed perceptions that his administration preferred a unilateral approach to dealing with problems. In 2006, for example, the university administration decided to remove an art exhibit featuring paintings by Palestinian children depicting scenes of violence in the Middle East. In response, a faculty-sponsored committee issued a statement of rebuke, claiming that university leadership made an "uncharacteristic error" by removing the artwork. Reinharz rebutted by saying only that faculty had raised "valid issues" and insisted that the entire university needed to just move on (Marder, 2006).

Despite a renewed period of success and growth, a perceived lack of transparency and limited opportunities for participation in university decision making continued to be part of the Brandeis experience. Although many faculty members, including some of his detractors, recognized the important contributions Reinharz made to the institution, there was a sense that past grievances were not forgotten or healed. It is in this climate that the Rose Art Museum crisis emerged in early 2009.

Setting the Stage for Crisis: A Lead Up to the Rose Closing Announcement

The beginnings of the Rose crisis began in a climate of great economic uncertainty. The stock market crash in the fall of 2008 abruptly ended an era of ballooning university endowments across higher education. By January 2009, the market continued a downward trend, and universities faced growing financial uncertainty. Brandeis was hampered in its response by a small and highly restricted endowment (Brandeis community member, personal communication, December 2, 2009). To complicate matters, Bernie Madoff's $50 billion ponzi scheme unraveled in December 2008. This disproportionately affected the Jewish philanthropic community, threatening one of Brandeis's most reliable supplementary revenue sources.

In January 2009, just prior to the announcement to close the museum, Brandeis acknowledged a 25 percent drop in its endowment and a $4 million shortfall for the current academic year. At the time, Executive Vice President and Chief Operating Officer Peter French was also quoted in *The Justice* estimating that the shortfall had the possibility of ballooning to $23 million by 2014 (Neubauer, 2009). Aware of the university's tenuous financial situation, the faculty voted unanimously on January 22, 2009, to support administrative efforts to address the economic recession. Anxiety on campus was high, but at this point leadership had yet to articulate a specific plan.

On January 26, 2009, the faculty and staff of Brandeis University received an official announcement from President Jehuda Reinharz (personal e-mail communication, January 26, 2009).

> Brandeis University's Board of Trustees today voted unanimously to close the Rose Art Museum as part of a campus-wide effort to preserve the university's educational mission in the face of the historic economic recession and financial crisis. . . . After necessary legal approvals and working with a top auction house, the university will publicly sell the art collection. Proceeds from the sale will be reinvested in the university to combat the far-reaching effects of the economic crisis, and fortify the university's position for the future.

An hour before the statement's release, Provost Marty Krauss notified the director of the Rose Art Museum, Michael Rush, that the museum was to be closed and the collection sold. Neither he nor the Rose Board of Directors were consulted with or informed of the plan at any time prior to the announcement. This was the first relay of information to occur outside of the administration's inner circle (Kennedy and Vogel, 2009).

The media, sensitive to the effects of the nation's deteriorating economy, latched on to the story. Local TV stations and the *Boston Globe* ran stories about the museum's closing. The following day, the story gained national exposure as the *New York Times* ran a report on the front page of its arts section (Kennedy and Vogel, 2009). Within days of the announcement, students and other university groups began to protest the decision.

As the days went on, the severity of the crisis intensified. On February 2, 2009, the *New York Times* ran an unflattering editorial criticizing the decision to close the museum. The piece observed that while "selling the university's art collection would help plug its financial gap, it would create a gaping hole in Brandeis's mission and reputation" ("Art at Brandeis," 2009). This harsh rebuke from a preeminent media outlet highlighted the severity and scope of the attention brought on by the decision.

The administration made efforts to contain the crisis, but these proved largely inadequate. On February 6, 2009, a conciliatory Reinharz backtracked from the initial administrative announcement, declaring that he regretted not finding "a more inclusive and open way to engage the

NEW DIRECTIONS FOR HIGHER EDUCATION • DOI: 10.1002/he

Brandeis community in the deliberations that led to the Board's decision" (personal e-mail communication, 2009b). The *mea culpa*, however, did not quell media attention surrounding the Rose crisis. Both the *Boston Globe* and the *New York Times* continued to give the story considerable attention.

In the following weeks, university leadership seemed unsure of the best way to respond to the public relations crisis. In a change of tactics, Reinharz emphasized in subsequent public statements that the Rose would continue to exist as a teaching facility and only a limited number of artworks would be sold, "if and when it is necessary" (Jan and Schworm, 2009). By reframing the issue, he also attempted to take direct responsibility for the decision and for the first time expressed regret for not reaching out to the community as part of the decision-making process. But to highlight the administration's concern over the scope of the crisis, they also chose to hire a public relations firm to help with the crisis management efforts (Kirsch, 2009).

The university gradually began to adopt a more open and consultative approach. On March 9, 2009, Provost Krauss authorized formation of a university-wide committee to make recommendations on the fate of the Rose Museum. The Future of the Rose Committee included faculty, students, alumni, a museum staff member, a member of the Rose Board of Overseers, and university trustee. This represents the first formal involvement of Brandeis community constituencies in the formal decision-making process (Rahman, 2009).

In September 2009, the Future of the Rose Committee issued its final report. It recommended that the museum remain open to the public and that it be better integrated into the core mission of the university. The report made no recommendations of the sale of art. The agnosticism was due in part to pending litigation. Despite the recommendation, Reinharz reiterated that the board's decision to auction off art remained on the table if necessary (Jan, 2009b).

A mere two days later, President Reinharz announced that he was stepping down as president effective in 2011. Although he maintains that the Rose was not a factor in his decision, it is widely speculated that the crisis played a part in his decision. As of July 2010, the university and supporters of the Rose Art Museum remain engaged in litigation to determine whether the university has the legal right to sell all or part of the collection. Trial dates have been set for December 2010. The university maintains that the decision to sell art remains on the table if necessary (Abramson, 2010).

Outcomes

As of July 2010, the Rose Art Museum remains open to the public, but the future of the museum and the collection remains uncertain. No artwork has been sold, but litigation disputing the right to sell the collection as an institutional asset is still pending (Edgers, 2010). The case may have larger implications for the art community and higher education if the courts weigh in on the Board of Trustees' authority to sell donor-provided assets as a means of offsetting operating expenses and budget deficits.

Brandeis's overall financial health is still in question. In February 2010 the school announced that it would undertake budget cuts to deal with a continued shortfall. It also suffered a credit rating downgrading by Moody's (Neubauer, 2010). The university also began a search for a new college president. The board has made efforts to reach out to its constituencies to participate in the process. The search committee, still in the process of deliberation, includes thirteen people: nine trustees, three faculty members, and one student representative (Abramson, 2009).

Organizational Tendencies: Sowing the Seeds for Crisis

A culture of strong presidential leadership may have contributed to a lack of situational awareness during the Rose Art Museum crisis. Corporate-style leadership was an assumed aspect of Brandeis University culture, but so too was anti-authority protest politics. Without mechanisms for encouraging consensus, internal divisions grew and collective action stalled precisely when it was needed most.

Whether the administration's decision was prudent in the context of the situation is irrelevant. A brief scan of Brandeis's history shows a pattern of administrative decision making that can be characterized as unaware or dismissive of existing organizational tensions. In the "Kosher" crisis of 1987, the Palestinian Art incident of 2006, and the Rose Art crisis of 2009, unilateral decision making from the board and top-down implementation without mechanisms for campus consultation, notification, and consent hurt leadership's ability to create and implement change.

It would be inaccurate, however, to describe Brandeis University as a place rife with division. In fact, throughout my research, I am struck by the core values that are deeply held by all aspects of the organization's component parts. Ambition, pride, and the drive for recognition and excellence permeate virtually every constituency and comprise core values central to the university's culture. Founded on a set of ambitious goals, subsequent iterations of leadership, faculty, students, staff, and donors have all embraced the high expectations initially set by Abram Sachar. Despite this unifying ethos, a lack of organizational cohesion has led to component parts as seeing itself with a unique stake in the future of Brandeis. Ironically, a shared vision fostered division as constituencies often disagreed on how to realistically implement lofty and ambitious goals.

Brandeis also suffers from a certain level of what scholar Victor Baldridge characterizes as "goal ambiguity" (1978, p. 20). Even in its early beginnings, university leaders had to simultaneously embrace the influence of Jewish cultural traditions while trying to disassociate itself from its Jewish identity. This idea of a dual identity continued to plague subsequent generations of campus community members. The search for the "soul" of the organization was not adequately defined from the outset. As a result, subsequent controversies have often focused on how the university defines its institutional mission and connections to society at large.

The result was an organization that suffered from a case of intense image anxiety. In the beginning, the success of the university was considered symbolic of Jewish influence in American society. As the university grew, it not only bore the hopes and expectations of the Board of Trustees, it also carried with it those of the Jewish community. This dual identity created a series of social mandates to embody excellence in education and culture. With the formation of the Rose Art Museum, the iconic presence of Leonard Bernstein, and the university's deep connections to the Jewish community, Brandeis found itself burdened by the expectations of multiple cultural communities. Although these commitments symbolized important indicators of the university's overall prestige, the resulting mandates proved difficult to balance while simultaneously tending to the university's core academic and financial responsibilities.

As a result of goal ambiguity, leadership, faculty, and students often angled to control the image of the university seen by the larger public. Through interviews and my personal experiences on campus, I get the sense that the university as a whole was, and still remains, sensitive to the perceptions of the university made by the outside world. This is particularly true concerning the negative media coverage it often receives. The characterization of Brandeis as a hotbed of student unrest earned during the tumultuous 1960s—whether deserved or not—has contributed heavily to its image-consciousness. Its unique place within the context of the ongoing Israel–Palestine debates served to only fuel these perceptions. The ingrained need for acceptance and recognition, along with the resulting insecurity that comes when outward reputation falls short of internal esteem, contributed to inter-organizational division and uncoordinated collective action.

Finally, the emphasis on growth and excellence pioneered by Sachar (and continued by Reinharz) has created an organizational culture that prides itself on expansion. This occurred despite a history of relative financial insecurity. As one professor put it, Brandeis is "a university with champagne ambitions operating on a beer budget" (as quoted in Jan, 2009a). As a result, Brandeis spent much of its financial resources on capital improvements, but also failed to prioritize the build-up of its endowment as a necessity for long-term success.

Together, these cultural factors created volatile relationships between various constituencies. Not all are negative; in fact, I am struck by the organization's shared sense of ambition and the value placed on excellence and prestige. However, without an overarching consensus on how the university should collectively move forward, internal organizational dynamics and accepted cultural norms have conspired to hinder its ability to present a united image and mission to the outside public.

NEW DIRECTIONS FOR HIGHER EDUCATION • DOI: 10.1002/he

Conclusion

The Brandeis Rose Art Museum crisis underscores the tensions that can exist between administrative leadership and the many parts of a complex university. Consensus across the organization and a collectively held sense of purpose are critical to decisive action in times of crisis. In the future, Brandeis leadership should consider ways to adopt a more collegial and consensus-oriented decision-making process. The corporate-style leadership that helped build a reputation for excellence also contributed to several incidents that tarnished the university's image. It remains true that consensus building can slow the decision-making process. However, if university leadership fails to adequately address student and faculty calls for a more meaningful role in this process, it will find internal divisions reinforced—and even exacerbated—at times when unified action is needed most.

References

Abramson, A. "Presidential Search Committee Hears Student Opinions." *The Brandeis Justice,* December. 1, 2009. Retrieved March 15, 2010, from http://www.thejusticeonline.com.

Abramson, A. "University Considering Alternative Options to Selling Art from Rose Collection."*The Brandeis Justice,* May 25, 2010. Accessed July 5, 2010 from http://www.thejusticeonline.com

"Art at Brandeis" [Editorial]. *The New York Times,* February 2, 2009, p. 20. Retrieved December 5, 2009, from http://www.nytimes.com

Baldridge, V. J., and others. "Organizational Characteristics of Colleges and Universities." In *Policy Making and Effective Leadership: A National Study of Academic Management.* San Francisco: Jossey-Bass, 1978, pp. 19–47.

Brandeis University. "Brandeis University: A People's History." Waltham, Mass.: Brandeis University, n.d. Retrieved December 6, 2009, from http://lts.brandeis.edu/research/archivesspeccoll/exhibits/b50/Timeline.

Edgers, G. "Ailing Brandeis Will Shut Museum, Sell Treasured Art: No Other Choice, Says President." *The Boston Globe,* January 27, 2010, p. A1.

Freeland, R. M. *Academia's Golden Age.* New York: Oxford University Press, 1992.

Jan, T. "Brandeis Woes Put President on the Line." *The Boston Globe,* February 18, 2009a, p. A1.

Jan, T. "Report Urges Brandeis to Keep Rose Open to the Public; Panel Doesn't Take Stand on Sale of Art." *The Boston Globe,* September 22, 2009b, Metro p. 3.

Jan, T., and Schworm, P. "Brandeis President Issues an Apology, Laments Museum Announcement." *The Boston Globe,* February 6, 2009, p. A1.

Kennedy, R., and Vogel, C. "Outcry Over a Plan to Sell Museum's Holdings." *The New York Times,* January 28, 2009, pp. C1.

Kirsch, H. "Disputes Continue Over Rose." *The Brandeis Justice,* March 10, 2009. Retrieved March 15, 2010, from from http:// www.thejusticeonline.com

Marder, R. "Faculty Critical of Art Removal: 'Move On,' Reinharz Says." *The Brandeis Justice,* October 10, 2009. Retrieved December 4, 2009, from http://www.thejustceonline.com

McLaughlin, J. B., and Reck, Rachel. "Teaching Case: Pork and Shellfish at Brandeis University." Cambridge, MA: Harvard University, 1997.

Neubauer, M. "French: Univ Endowment Down 25 Percent, Budget Gap Projected to Grow to $23 Million by 2014." *The Brandeis Justice,* January 27, 2009. Retrieved December 7, 2009, from http:// www.thejusticeonline.com

Neubauer, M. "Credit Agency Lowers Rating of Brandeis Due to Finances." *The Brandeis Justice*, March 2, 2010. Retrieved March 7, 2010, from http://www.thejustice online.com

Rahman, N. "Committee on the Future of the Rose Art Museum Releases Final Report." *The Brandeis Justice*, September 22, 2009. Retrieved December 5, 2009, from http://www.thejusticeonline.com

Rush, M. *The Rose Art Museum at Brandeis*. New York: Abrams, 2009.

Shworm, P. "Brandeis President to Step Down: Says Rose Outcry Didn't Affect Move." *The Boston Globe*, September 25, 2009. Retrieved on December 6, 2009, from http://www.bostonglobe.com

Wald. M. "At Brandeis, Ham, Steak, and Shrimp." *The New York Times*, September 11, 1987, p. A16.

PAUL DILLON *is a recent graduate of the Ed.M. in Higher Education program from the Harvard Graduate School of Education.*

NEW DIRECTIONS FOR HIGHER EDUCATION • DOI: 10.1002/he

9

A new president finds himself at odds with defining traditions of his institution.

A Contested Institutional Culture

Stephanie A. Morin

The College of William and Mary (Williamsburg, Va.) found itself at a cross-roads in 2005. Their long-popular president Timothy J. Sullivan was retiring after thirteen years at the helm of the world's second oldest institution of higher education (Petkofsky, 2004). Long known as a bastion of conservatism, William and Mary could now change their future course through their newest presidential appointment. The school heeded this opportunity in their final selection of Gene R. Nichol. Nichol, a liberal democrat and former candidate for political office, won over the students, faculty, and Board of Visitors with his larger-than-life presence and impassioned speeches (Petkofsky, 2005).

As expected, Nichol attempted sweeping changes at William and Mary from the very outset of his tenure, but these initiatives were not met with widespread acclaim as many had anticipated. In the end, Nichol served as president for a mere two and a half years (Mahoney, 2008a). His tenure was a time of tumult and upheaval, and the culture and traditions of the college were rocked in many ways. This chapter presents the difficulties inherent in altering campus culture by looking first-hand at Nichol's struggles against institutional norms at William and Mary. Nichol's experiences highlight the necessity of understanding and integrating into an institution's culture and incorporating input from multiple constituencies to affect change successfully.

National College Athletic Association Logo

Nichol's struggle to understand and show deference to William and Mary's cultural identity began immediately. In 2004 the National College Athletic Association (NCAA) requested that William and Mary and other member organizations with mascots and logos containing Native American imagery complete a self-evaluation to determine whether such items were hostile or

NEW DIRECTIONS FOR HIGHER EDUCATION, no. 151, Fall 2010 © Wiley Periodicals, Inc.
Published online in Wiley Online Library (wileyonlinelibrary.com) • DOI: 10.1002/he.404

abusive to Native peoples. Nichol inherited the task of defending William and Mary's athletic team name, "The Tribe," and the logo containing two feathers surrounding the initials "WM" ("College of William and Mary Receives NCAA Ruling," 2006). Nichol used the school's historic connection to the Native American populations in and around the Williamsburg colony to defend the team name and logo. He argued that "Tribe" reflected the "ennobling sentiments of commitment, shared idealism, community and common cause" (Walker, 2005, para. 1). The NCAA accepted this defense of the team name but in May 2006 outlawed the logo. The school appealed the ruling in July with the NCAA executive committee, but the appeal was denied in August. Nichol, in consultation with the Board, decided not to sue the NCAA and press the issue further, even though he stated that he found the decision and the NCAA's actions "galling" (Fisher, 2006, letter, para. 4). Nichol explained that a lawsuit would jeopardize athletes' ability to compete in coming years, would divert limited financial resources to a prolonged legal battle, and would tarnish William and Mary's reputation (Fisher, 2006).

The loss of the college's much-loved feathered logo marked the beginning of William and Mary's battle over campus identity. As Mark Connolly (2000) in the article, "What's In a Name" writes, "Athletic nicknames and logos are powerful cultural symbols because they not only evoke allegiance to an institution's athletic teams but also may be instrumental in shaping the image of the entire college or university" (p. 1). Nichol's decision not to fight to keep this important marker of William and Mary identity alienated many in the campus community who felt he did not value or understand the school's culture.

Once students and alumni adapted to the reality that the classic logo could no longer be used, they began to embrace the opportunity for an interesting new design. Nichol charged a task force of students, faculty, staff and alumni to create a new logo (Cota, 2008). Ultimately, when the new logo was revealed students and alumni were disappointed with what they saw as a lackluster effort. A staff editorial in the student newspaper stated that the committee had failed in its mission to "consolidate the history and identity of the College" ("New Logo a Disappointment," 2007, para. 6) and that the school "still lack[ed] a proper symbol" (para. 8). The loss of the logo and the uninspiring new design marked the beginning of anti-Nichol sentiment over issues of campus culture, which would grow exponentially during his tenure.

Gateway William and Mary

Nichol also came into conflict with the complex shared governance model of higher education in his efforts to address campus diversity. Just one week after his inauguration, Nichol stated that "the College needs to more vigorously open its doors to become more racially and geographically diverse" (Cota, 2008, para. 3). To achieve this goal, Nichol instituted the Gateway

William and Mary program, an initiative to provide a debt-free education to students from low-income families. The idea for the program began under Nichol's predecessor, but Nichol took the idea from its nascent stages into preliminary implementation. Although the Board and others at the college supported the idea behind the program, many criticized Nichol's hastiness. He failed to consult the Board and other campus leaders prior to implementing the program. The amount of funding necessary for the program to be successful required, in the short-term, a major reallocation of the school's budget and, in the long-term, a substantial fundraising effort. Nichol responded to his detractors, arguing that if the program had demonstrated success it would be easier to raise the necessary funds (Mahoney, 2008b).

Other constituencies, however, had different views about the proper course of action. John Kotter and Leonard Schlesinger (1979) in the article "Choosing Strategies for Change" argue that subordinates often resist change when they perceive greater costs to the endeavor than benefits. Furthermore, leaders and followers are often operating with different sets of information, which colors their opinions regarding change. Nichol believed that positive press surrounding the creation of Gateway would be enough to gain financial momentum; however, from the Board and faculty's perspective the immediate reorganization of the college's budget created significant short-term costs. A faculty representative stated, "Much of the opposition to Gateway has nothing to do with ideology but instead rests on a disagreement about how to spend the College's very scarce resources" (Mahoney, 2008b). Kotter and Schlesinger (1979) argue that an effective way of avoiding this type of resistance is to involve constituents in the implementation of change. Nichol acted hastily to implement Gateway and failed to consult broadly with the organization's insiders. He would make similar missteps again during his presidency, resulting in increased resistance to his leadership.

The Wren Cross Controversy

In October 2006, after reports that the presence of a small, brass altar cross in the college's historic Wren Chapel had offended non-Christian students, Nichol unilaterally removed the cross from permanent display. The cross was donated to the school in 1940 by the local Bruton Parish Church in Williamsburg to commemorate William and Mary's founding as an institution of the Anglican Church. Although now a state university, the Wren Chapel is still used for religious services and is an integral part of the William and Mary history and culture. A policy concerning the cross stated that it could be removed at the request of those holding events in the chapel (Godson, 2006).

Nichol did not immediately inform the campus community, but news of the cross's removal began to spread when the assistant historical director of the Wren Building sent an e-mail regarding the change to student tour guide volunteers ("Assistant Historical Director," 2006). As various rumors swirled, Nichol sent an e-mail to all students explaining that the chapel is often used for secular events and should be open and welcoming to all religious backgrounds. Nichol also urged the campus community to contemplate and debate about the role of the Wren Chapel in the William and Mary community ("Gene Nichol's Email Confirming Order," 2006).

Debate began almost immediately. Student, faculty, and alumni opinion was mixed. Some were offended religiously by the removal of a Christian object from its place on an altar, while many non-Christians supported Nichol's decision, saying that they now felt welcome in the chapel ("Nichol Discusses Wren Cross," 2006). Others focused not on the religious dimension of the decision but the historical and cultural importance of the cross and the chapel. An alumnus argued: "If Nichol's cross-removal order stands, the W&M community will be accepting a dramatic erosion of its core historic identity. The Wren Chapel and cross honor W&M's historic mission contained in the college's 1693 Royal Charter to train young men for Christian ministry" (Haley, 2006).

Nichol failed to understand the centrality of history and tradition in the William and Mary culture prior to his decision. As Harry Petersen (2008) argues in *Leading a Small College or University: A Conversation That Never Ends,* "A president's effective leadership requires an understanding of what motivates the organization's people and shapes their behavior. . . . Failing to understand their organization's culture causes many presidents to founder" (p. 34). It was not until after the controversy erupted that Nichol understood the depth of emotion involved in his decision.

In an e-mail following the initial upheaval, Nichol acknowledged the cultural dimension of the controversy, stating, "Many. . .have worried that, as a new president, I have failed to understand and sufficiently value the storied traditions of the College" (Pinkerton, 2006, letter, para. 8). The fact that Nichol had been the College's president for less than a year and a half when he decided to alter the way the cross was displayed gave the impression that an outsider was coming into the community and imposing values that were not the organization's.

Nichol was criticized not only for his lack of understanding of the William and Mary culture, but for failing to seek input from campus constituencies. An editorial in the student newspaper read: "Despite the obvious importance of this decision, it was made unexpectedly and without debate. There was no indication from the president that he was considering changing a half-century-old tradition, nor any consultation with the thousands of William and Mary students, professors and alumni who consider the Wren Building a symbolic embodiment of the college they hold so dear. The complete dismissal of community opinion is disrespectful to our traditions and ideals, and it has stirred up a deep well of resentment. (Anonymous, 2006, para. 2)

Similarly, Vince Haley, a graduate of the class of 1988, was offended by the lack of broad consultation. He was so angered that he registered the domain name www.SaveTheWrenCross.org and began mobilizing students, alumni, and religious organizations throughout the country to oppose Nichol's actions. A key aspect of the Web site was a petition calling on Nichol to rescind the policy change (Petkofsky, 2006a). By the quarterly meeting of the Board in November, the petition had received 1,400 signatories. At the meeting, Nichol reiterated his reasons for removing the cross and stood behind his decision. Furthermore, the Board reaffirmed their overall faith in Nichol's leadership, despite the mounting controversy (Petkofsky, 2006b).

Protests continued, however, and Nichol was forced to reevaluate his original policy change. In an e-mail to the campus community on December 20, Nichol explained that the college would commission a plaque to be placed permanently in the Wren Chapel commemorating the college's Christian roots. He also stated that the cross would be displayed every Sunday and would be used at all Christian events, and that any event organizer could request the cross be displayed (Pinkerton, 2006). Despite Nichol's e-mail, tensions multiplied. Vince Haley continued to attract signatures to his online petition, and he supplemented his Web site with editorials in newspapers across Virginia. By January 17, 2007, Haley's petition had attracted more than 9,000 signatories (Petkofsky, 2007).

Nichol addressed the mounting controversy in his State of the College address in January. He announced the creation of the Committee on Religion in a Public University to articulate a new policy for the Wren Cross and to facilitate an examination of broader issues of religion at a public university. The committee was composed of fourteen members, including two student representatives and a mixture of alumni, faculty, and administrators. In this way, Nichol was responding to his numerous critics that he had acted unilaterally (Cochrane, 2007a).

The Virginia General Assembly also began to express their opinions on Nichol's leadership. In February, a delegate presented a motion to eliminate the state's contribution to Nichol's salary, effectively cutting his compensation in half, if the cross were not returned by May 3. The motion failed, but the final vote of fifty-eight to thirty-six reflected the near split opinion of the state legislature (Hardy, 2007).

The controversy culminated in February when news spread that James McGlothlin, a college and law school graduate and a former Board member, had withdrawn a $12 million pledge in the wake of the Wren Cross scandal (Wright, 2007a). Nichol had just announced the early completion of a seven-year, $500 million fundraising campaign; however, the withdrawn pledge knocked the college back below the $500 million benchmark. Allegations swirled that Nichol was aware of the withdrawn pledge prior to his announcement and that he had knowingly misrepresented the campaign

NEW DIRECTIONS FOR HIGHER EDUCATION • DOI: 10.1002/he

totals. His opponents continued to reference the lost donation and argue that Nichol lied to the campus community (Wright, 2007c).

In March, the Committee on Religion in a Public University issued their unanimous recommendation to the Board and President Nichol. They recommended that the cross be permanently returned to the Wren Chapel and kept in a glass display case with a plaque commemorating the school's Anglican roots and connection with the Bruton Parish Church (Wright, 2007b). The cross would not be returned to the altar, but displayed near the east entrance door (Cochrane, 2007b). In this way it would serve as an historic symbol and not a religious symbol. The committee also determined that the chapel sacristy should be available to house sacred objects from any religious tradition. The committee's recommendation was embraced by Nichol, the Board, www.SaveTheWrenCross.org, and other activist groups (Wright, 2007b).

Nichol's problems did not cease with the conclusion of the Wren Cross controversy, however. Constituency groups' opinions about his leadership had already solidified, and all of his actions were now carefully scrutinized. Controversy erupted again in the spring of 2007 when a racy performance art group appeared on campus.

The Sex Workers' Art Show

The Sex Workers' Art Show, a traveling performance featuring former and current employees of the sex industry, had visited campus before, but was not heavily advertised. The show garnered more widespread attention in spring 2007 when a professor, seeing a poster announcing the event, contacted the *Virginia Gazette*. Nichol allowed the event to continue despite calls for its cancellation stating, "it's not the practice and province of universities to censor or cancel performances because they are controversial" (Cota, 2007, para. 2). When the Sex Workers' Art Show was slated to appear in spring 2008 and Nichol again refused to cancel the event, controversy boiled over (Guillen, 2008b). On the heels of the Wren Cross media frenzy, members of the campus community and beyond began to question the morals evinced on campus (Broskie, 2008; Guillen, 2008b).

In response to the criticism, Board Chairman Michael Powell issued a statement supporting Nichol and stating, "we have faith that our students have the wisdom to put such programming in context if they choose to attend the show" (Guillen, 2008a). Although there was some student opposition to the presence of the show, it was minimal. Two performances were completely sold out in the 450 seat auditorium, and only about twenty-five students showed up to protest (Guillen, 2008b).

Despite minimal opposition to the Sex Workers' Art Show within the campus's walls, public perception of Nichol in the media continued to suffer. Opponents overstated the matters characterizing Nichol as for sex and against religion, and the debate began to take on a political aspect. Nichol's liberal political background became a focal point for his opponents, who were mainly conservatives. News editorials, letters, and blog posts following the removal of the cross illuminated the prevailing sentiment among many conservatives that Nichol's personal politics did not fit within the William and Mary culture. The Board had expressed reserve about Nichol's political past during the presidential search. Ultimately, under assurances from Nichol that his politics would not play a role in William and Mary's leadership, they overlooked his background as a liberal activist (Petkofsky, 2005). Nichol later acknowledged the cultural and political dimension to his presidency, stating, "I was treated to a potent dose of cultural contest. . . . I've seen at close hand the impact that battling bloggers, right-wing donors, fevered Fox News firebrands, demagogic legislators and trustees unschooled in and uncommitted to the core values of a university can have upon a presidency and an institution. They are nothing to scoff at" (Nichol, 2008b).

It was in this fervent environment that the Board began the customary review of Nichol's tenure in September 2007 to assess whether his contract, set to expire at the end of the 2007–2008 school year, would be renewed.

Non-renewal and Resignation

In their review, the Board sought input from faculty, staff, students, alumni, and friends of the college, but emphasized that the decision was not up to a referendum and would be the ultimate purview of the Board ("W&M Takes Comments," 2007). Many alumni, donors, and students expressed their opinions about Nichol's tenure (Todor, 2007). The contract renewal debate extended to the state government, as well. Then-Governor of Virginia Timothy Kaine had made three new appointments to the Board when the state legislature was not in session, and those appointments had to be confirmed by lawmakers. In February 2008, in the midst of the ongoing review, the three Board members up for confirmation were summoned by the Chairman of the House Privileges and Elections Committee, Mark Cole, to comment on Nichol's review and the events at William and Mary. Cole and other delegates specifically mentioned concerns over the continued presence of the Sex Workers' Art Show and the handling of the Wren Cross controversy (Meola, 2008).

After months of debate the Board informed Nichol on February 10, 2008, that they would not renew his contract after it expired at the end of the school year. The first word that the campus community received of this decision came from Nichol on February 12, 2008. Nichol resigned his post as president effective immediately in an e-mail to students, faculty, and staff, claiming that he was dismissed for ideological reasons. Nichol listed four reasons for his non-renewal: the Wren Cross controversy, the Sex Workers' Art Show, the Gateway program and the growing diversity on campus. Beyond this, he argued that Mark Cole and other members of the Virginia House of Delegates had threatened the Board appointees in calling them to

Richmond if he were not fired. Nichol also accused the Board of bribing him to remain quiet over his dismissal. He wrote, "The Board offered both my wife and me substantial economic incentives if we would agree 'not to characterize [the non-renewal decision] as based on ideological grounds' or make any other statement about my departure without their approval. . .It would have required that I make statements I believe to be untrue and that I believe most would find non-credible. I've said before that the values of the College are not for sale. Neither are ours" (Nichol, 2008a).

Nichol's resignation and claims sparked an immediate frenzy, with Nichol's detractors celebrating the Board's decision and his supporters lobbing various accusations.

Due to the uproar, the Board held a series of meetings with faculty, staff, and students to defend their stance on Nichol's presidency and answer questions. They insisted that their decision was based on failings in Nichol's executive leadership and offered several examples of his shortcomings. First, Chairman Powell said that the Gateway William and Mary program was on the verge of failing due to lack of funding. The Board had advised Nichol to hire a chief operating officer for the program over a year ago and Nichol failed to heed the suggestion. The Board denied Nichol's accusation that his attempts to diversify the college both racially and socioeconomically were an impetus for his dismissal. They reiterated that they supported his efforts and would like to see Gateway continued if funding could be secured. Second, Powell stated that although the Board agreed with Nichol's stance on the Wren Cross and the Sex Workers' Art Show, they were bothered by the lack of communication Nichol exhibited in regards to these incidents. Nichol failed to inform the Board of the mounting controversies, leaving them to hear about the developments through the media (Geroux, 2008). Finally, Powell argued that the Board did not bribe Nichol into silence, but offered him a customary severance package to help his transition to future employment. He explained that the Board's intention was not to censor Nichol, but to negotiate an appropriate public statement that would allow both the institution and Nichol to move forward with dignity (Wright, 2008).

Conclusion

The events that occurred at William and Mary from 2005 to 2008 were small battles in a culture war. Nichol ultimately became a casualty of a complex organizational culture composed of multiple stakeholders. As we have seen, faculty and student opinion were mixed in regards to Nichol's leadership. Similarly, although the Board seemed to back Nichol through his toughest battles, they could not ignore the overwhelming opposition that alumni, donors, and the state legislature voiced. In the book *Legitimacy in the Academic Presidency*, Rita Bornstein (2003) notes that discord among a college's constituents often forces the board to reconsider the president's place in the institution. She writes, "The search for cultural adaptation and acceptance is a mutual process between the new president and the institution's constituents. Most presidents work hard to learn and adapt to their new culture. Some, generally to their peril, turn their backs on the institution's history and traditions as they seek to make change. And, on occasion, despite a president's best efforts, significant groups of faculty, alumni, or trustees will not accept the new leader as their own" (p. 45).

Nichol's struggles against key William and Mary stakeholders in responding to the NCAA logo ban, establishing the Gateway William and Mary program, and navigating the Wren Cross and Sex Workers' Art Show controversies evidence Bornstein's assertion. Nichol's presidency illuminates the difficulties inherent in altering a campus culture and navigating multiple constituencies. It is possible to institute change at a college, even one with as much tradition and history as William and Mary, but change often happens slowly and requires broad consultation and deference to the organization's values.

References

Anonymous. "Editorial: Nichol Botched Handling of Cross." *The Flat Hat,* December 7, 2006. Retrieved December 9, 2009, from http://flathatnews.com
"Assistant Historical Director's Email Announcing the Decision" Web log post, October 2006. Message posted to http://www.savethewrencross.org/melissasemail.php
Bornstein, R. *Legitimacy in the Academic Presidency*. Westport, Conn.: Praeger Publishers, 2003.
Broskie, C. "William and Mary President's Resignation Sparks Controversy." *The Commonwealth Times*, February 25, 2008. Retrieved December 5, 2009, from http://www.com monwealthtimes.com
Cochrane, A. "Nichol Unveils Religion Committee." *The Flat Hat*, February 20, 2007a. Retrieved December 5, 2009, from http://flathatnews.com
Cochrane, A. "Cross Placement Decided." *The Flat Hat*, April 17, 2007b. Retrieved December 5, 2009, from http://flathatnews.com
"College of William and Mary Receives NCAA Ruling on Athletic Logo." Williamsburg, Va.: The College of William and Mary Office of University Relations, August 3, 2006. Retrieved December 5, 2009, from http://web.wm.edu/news/archive/index.php?id=6369
Connolly, M. R. "What's in a Name?: A Historical Look at Native American-Related Nicknames and Symbols at Three U.S. Universities." *The Journal of Higher Education*, 2000, 71(5), 515–547.
Cota, A. "Nichol Turned Off by Campus Sex Art Show." *The Flat Hat*, February 16, 2007. Retrieved November 27, 2009, from http://flathatnews.com
Cota, A. "For Nichol, a Mixed Legacy." *The Flat Hat*, February 14, 2008. Retrieved December 5, 2009, from http://flathatnews.com
Fisher, M. "Hostile and Abusive Feathers" [Web log post, October 12, 2006]. Message posted to http://voices.washingtonpost.com/rawfisher/2006/10/hostile_and_abu sive_feathers.html
"Gene Nichol's Email Confirming Order to Remove Cross from Wren Chapel" [Web log post, October 27, 2006]. Message posted to http://www.savethewrencross.org/nicholse mail.php

Geroux, B. "W&M Board Answers Critics; In Series of Meetings, Members Try to Explain Why Nichol Was Let Go." *Richmond Times Dispatch,* February 23, 2008, p. A1.

Godson, S. "Re: History of the Wren Cross" [Online forum comment, November 11, 2006]. Message posted to http://www.savethewrencross.org/brutonletter.php

Guillen, A. "The Sex Show A Go-Go." *The Flat Hat,* January 29, 2008a. Retrieved November 27, 2009, from http://flathatnews.com

Guillen, A. "Sex, Art, Outrage." *The Flat Hat,* February 5, 2008b. Retrieved November 27, 2009, from http://flathatnews.com

Haley, V. "The Wren Chapel Cross Controversy; William and Mary Displays New Intolerance." *Richmond Times Dispatch,* November 20, 2006, p. A11.

Hardy, M. "Pros, Cons of Wren Cross in Richmond; House Votes Against Cutting Nichol's Salary; It Supports Board Review." *Richmond Times Dispatch,* February 9, 2007, p. B1.

Kotter, J. P., and Schlesinger, L. A. "Choosing Strategies for Change." *Harvard Business Review,* 1979, 57(2), 106–114.

Mahoney, B. "Nichol Resigns, Ending Shortest Presidency since Civil War." *The Flat Hat,* February 15, 2008a. Retrieved December 9, 2000, from http://flathatnews.com

Mahoney, B. "Controversy Surrounds Gateway." *The Flat Hat,* February 27, 2008b. Retrieved November 27, 2009, from http://flathatnews.com

Meola, O. "W&M Board Members Called to Richmond; Delegate Concerned after Controversies over Sex Show, Cross." *Richmond Times Dispatch,* February 6, 2008, p. A6.

"New Logo a Disappointment." *The Flat Hat,* December 7, 2007. Retrieved December 5, 2009 from http://flathatnews.com

"Nichol Discusses Wren Cross Decision with BOV" [Web log post, November 20, 2006]. Message posted to http://www.savethewrencross.org/bovtext.php

Nichol, G. R. "February 12, 2008 Letter to Members of the William and Mary Community." Retrieved November 27, 2009, from http://www.washingtonpost.com/wp-srv/metro/pdfs/letter_nichol021208.pdf?sid=ST2008021201428 and http://www.washingtonpost.com/wp-dyn/content/story/2008/02/12/ST2008021201428.html

Nichol, G. R. "Public Universities at Risk Abandoning Their Mission" [Review of the book *Unmaking the Public University: The Forty-Year Assault on the Middle Class*]. *The Chronicle of Higher Education,* 2008, 55(10), 27.

Peterson, H. L. *Leading a Small College or University: A Conversation That Never Ends.* Madison, Wis.: Atwood Publishing, 2008.

Petkofsky, A. "Sullivan Resigning W&M Presidency/After Decade-Plus, He Says He Can Best Serve College by Leaving It." *Richmond Times Dispatch,* June 19, 2004, p. A1.

Petkofsky, A. "W&M President Breaks Mold; Selection of Liberal Nichol to Head Staid School a Novel Choice." *Richmond Times Dispatch,* September 19, 2005, p. A1.

Petkofsky, A. "Petition: Help Save W&M's Wren Cross; Discussion Is Lively as Bid Is Launched to Return Relic to Chapel." *Richmond Times Dispatch,* November 9, 2006a, p. B2.

Petkofsky, A. "W&M President Reiterated Reasons for Cross Removal." *Richmond Times Dispatch,* November 17, 2006b, p. B1.

Petkofsky, A. "W&M Plans Events on Chapel's Cross." *Richmond Times Dispatch,* January 17, 2007, p. B4.

Pinkerton, J. "Nichol Announces Changes to Wren Cross Policy." *The Flat Hat,* December 20, 2006. Retrieved November 27, 2009, from http://flathatnews.com

Todor, A. "Some 'Heart' Nichol, Others Hate." *The Flat Hat,* September 7, 2007. Retrieved December 9, 2009, from http://flathatnews.com

Walker, B. "'Tribe' Refers to Community Nichol States in a Report to the NCAA." Williamsburg, Va.: *The College of William and Mary Office of University Relations,* November 3, 2005. Retrieved December 8, 2009, from http://web.wm.edu/news/archive/index.php?id=5338

"W&M Takes Comments on Nichol's Performance." *Richmond Times Dispatch*, September 29, 2007, p. B8.

Wright, A. "Donor Pulls $12 Million over Wren Cross Policy." *The Flat Hat*, February 28, 2007a. Retrieved December 5, 2009, from http://flathatnews.com

Wright, A. "Cross to be Permanently Displayed in Wren Chapel." *The Flat Hat*, March 6, 2007b. Retrieved December 5, 2009, from http://flathatnews.com

Wright, A. "Questions Surface about Lost $12 Mil." *The Flat Hat*, October 23, 2007c. Retrieved December 8, 2009, from http://flathatnews.com

Wright, A. "BOV Rector Discusses Nichol's Resignation with the Flat Hat." *The Flat Hat*, February 12, 2008. Retrieved November 27, 2009, from http://flathatnews.com

STEPHANIE A. MORIN *is a 2010 graduate of the Harvard Graduate School of Education.*

NEW DIRECTIONS FOR HIGHER EDUCATION • DOI: 10.1002/he

10

An accumulation of events can force a presidential transition.

Rapid Change and Legitimacy

Matthew Waldman

Nelson College, a rural community and technical college in the Midwest, serves roughly 5,600 students in over sixty degree and certification programs. As a part of the institution's mission, Nelson College offers a hands-on, open enrollment education that leads to employment and economic growth within the region. In attempting to serve this purpose, the school has many ties to local and regional organizations and serves as major part of economic development plans within the region.

Part I: Unraveling the Presidency

John Bowen had an unprecedented term as president, serving forty years from the founding of the college until the summer of 2009. Combined with his ability to identify trends, Bowen's brave leadership fostered growth and innovation. Joe Woodsman, who served as an Associate Dean under Bowen, spoke of the duality of his management style; with little regard for the consequences of decisions, college administrators were creative in solving complex problems and felt they were less confined in their role than peers at other institutions. However, decisions made without clear understanding and communication often frustrated campus constituencies. Woodsman added, "for all the good points, the bravado also led to chaos and a lack of quality control."

Leadership Culture at Nelson College. The amount of risk that John Bowen assumed during his leadership was a direct result of his longevity. One of the key figures in the founding of the organization, Bowen helped

---

Nelson College, as well as the names of its faculty and administration, are pseudonyms used to protect the identity of the college and its community.

New Directions for Higher Education, no. 151, Fall 2010 © Wiley Periodicals, Inc.
Published online in Wiley Online Library (wileyonlinelibrary.com) • DOI: 10.1002/he.405

craft the members of the Board of Trustees. During his presidency, the members gave unquestioned support to the executive office. When the state capitol newspaper published articles concerning the legality of Bowen's political contributions, the board gave him a contract extension in defiance of the public allegations (E. Robinson, November 23, 2009, personal communication).

Similarly, Bowen's senior management team had a personal interest in the president's success. Some high-level administrators maintain that the employees attained their executive posts from their years of experience at the college; others contend that their close friendships with Bowen seemed to lead to positions in senior management (K. Lowe, November 24, 2009, personal communication). Most dramatically, Bowen promoted his wife, who had worked in several administrative functions at the school, to vice president of student affairs.

An official in the provost's office states that many feel he surrounded himself with a buffer of personal relationships (K. Lowe, November 24, 2009, personal communication). Woodsman goes as far as to call Bowen's leadership team "inbred," and states that Bowen and his team were able to make decisions without accountability or transparency. He added, "Besides the board, who rarely raised any objections, the people in a position to call for accountability were benefiting from the system" (J. Woodsman, November 23, 2009, personal communication).

From this perspective, the senior-level management had developed a cohesive cognitive bias, which relied upon the acceptance of ideas found mutually beneficial to the decision-making party. Good decision making often arrives from a synthesis of different perspectives, demanding both advocacy and inquiry (M. Higgins, personal communication, November 10, 2009). Without a dissenting opinion, policies can be made and called to action without inquiry or transparency. An anonymous employee used the phrase "management by whimsy" to describe the rationale behind these decisions: "Anything that [senior management] found interesting or enjoyable became a priority" (Anonymous #1, personal communication, November 24, 2009).

His supporters argue that the collegiate atmosphere in senior management brought a culture of psychological safety that inspired innovation. One administrator claims that many of Nelson College's successes were a direct result of respect and friendship between Bowen and his management team (Anonymous #2, personal communication, December 2, 2009).

Although there is validity to the concept that psychological safety and a collegial atmosphere produce innovative concepts, it is crucial to include accountability into the organizational model. Higgins suggests that high-performing organizations have both high levels of satisfaction and safety in the workplace and accountability for challenging goals (M. Higgins, personal communication, November 12, 2009). In adhering to this leadership principle, the institution's management is able to encourage a learning culture—willing to challenge their previous work and normative processes, promote innovative problem solving that requires follow-up explanations, and ultimately inspire employees through professional development.

Barbara French. Barbara French's marriage to the president made her promotion highly controversial and subject to discussion. Though Bowen had appointed many close friends to offices during his tenure, Lowe pointed to the perceptions that came with the promotion, "Regardless of whether she deserved the job, it hurt the college." The fallout from perceived cronyism and nepotism goes beyond the cognitive biases mentioned previously by sending a message that "getting ahead" is not based upon your professional effort, but on your relationship to the executive office. Within the admissions office at Nelson College, some described a sense of futility that overcame the young professionals hired to attract students to the open-enrollment institution. "People were showing up late for work, taking long lunches, and weren't meeting their [recruitment] goals" (Anonymous #1, personal communication, November 24, 2009). Without strong incentives tied to performance measures, enrollment at Nelson College stagnated, fluctuating above and below 5,500 students each academic quarter from 1995–2007 (National Center for Education Statistics, Integrated Postsecondary Education Data System, 2002).

Divisions in the Workplace. Prior to French's appointment, the Dean of Academic Affairs had long been vying for the vice presidency. The competition brought a division between the two senior administrators. The division led to a bitter feud between French and the dean that played out on campus for nearly a decade. The effects hurt the college's academic mission as French utilized her relationship with the president to garner the majority of the college's resources, leaving little for the academic units. K. Lowe (November 24, 2009 personal communication) spoke directly about the discrepancy, "I originally worked in student services and received a healthy budget for every project. I got a new laptop every other year. When I switched to academic affairs, I noticed the computers were older than the carpets in my old office. My first conference with Academic Affairs I shared a hotel room with the dean and we had [senior administrators] sleeping on cots. With student affairs we got our own room and even had upgrades."

External Conflict. Nelson College has a mission to serve the local and regional community as a center for economic growth. Inherent in this is the importance of public relations. Under the presidency of John Bowen, Nelson College provided a variety of well-received resources to the region. The most treasured and utilized is Lake Gunderson, which offers educational opportunities to the college's students and recreation to the local community. During the last years of Bowen's presidency, events occurred that undermined the college's role in the local community and placed his executive office in a bad light.

Lake Gunderson. Bowen's first major public relations gaffe was in the proposed sale of the already contentious, yet beloved, Lake Gunderson. Nelson College purchased the 651-acre plot from a municipal water conservancy,

NEW DIRECTIONS FOR HIGHER EDUCATION • DOI: 10.1002/he

the Local Creek Conservancy District, which had assumed the land under eminent domain and forced the sale on poor farming families during the 1960s. Regardless, the lake's use as a local fishing and camping spot provided little room for public upheaval. Later, Nelson College was able to purchase the land with little protest as they planned to keep it available as a community resource while adding laboratories for student learning.

Eight years into the college's ownership, they announced plans to sell part of the land to a local developer to create a resort on the property. Though the college claimed it was no longer able to financially support the property, community members became angry about the sale of land that had been taken from families still residing in the community. Others were offended by a variety of issues, from plans for the resort to sell alcohol in a "dry" county, and decreased access to the lake, to the capitalist nature of the proposed actions. Many in the area voiced their opinion on local radio shows, in newspapers and in heated town hall debates. In the end, legal roadblocks and public interest derailed the college's plan for the sale (Claussen, 2006).

As the face of Nelson College, and one of the main proponents behind the sale of Lake Gunderson, Bowen took a significant hit in public perception. Joe Woodsman recalls a published newspaper article insinuating that Bowen was to personally gain from the sale of the land. In his opinion, irreversible damage was done to Bowen's presidency (J. Woodsman, November 23, 2009, personal communication).

Legal Battles. In May of 2006 several Nelson College administrators were required to provide depositions before the State's Attorney General's Office regarding President Bowen's use of federal and state funds. The meetings, which took place at the county courthouse, were kept private, but word leaked to President Bowen, the trustees, and the senior management team, who accused them of meeting with local and state prosecutors to try and remove Bowen from the presidency. Staff and faculty rumors swirled about President Bowen's alleged illegal activity and many felt compelled to choose a side in the fight (Anonymous #2, December 2, 2009).

The media seemed to focus on only one aspect of the investigation—an executive meeting outside the United States. Lowe maintains that this merely diverted the public's attention from the true nature of the investigation (personal communication, November 24, 2009). Regardless, the story served as a powerful force in questioning Bowen's ability as president.

The End. The presidency of John Bowen came to an end, unceremoniously, when his contract expired on June 30, 2009, though the seeds of his exit had been planted over time. The truth behind Bowen's exit lies in the complex interweaving of three components.

Within Nelson College, Bowen had surrounded himself with a like-minded cohort that relieved one another from scrutiny. He created a culture that required little accountability in an era that calls for open access to information. To some constituencies, it appeared that Bowen and his management team were not prepared to justify nor share their rationale for decisions. Furthermore, the promotion of his wife into the vice presidency may have added resentment and distrust from faculty and staff at the college.

Meanwhile, the dissolving partnership between Nelson College and the community produced two results. First, media sources looked for reasons to provide the public with supporting evidence for their mistrust. Second, the constant media inquiry affected the morale of Nelson's employees. If staff and faculty support was already questionable, the bad press added to the questionability of Bowen's ability to serve as president (Anonymous #1, November 24, 2009).

When the government began its investigation into the misuse of funds, it combined internal and external mistrust of the presidency into a complete call for action. Media allegations provided dissenters with the confidence to openly question Bowen's leadership. As a result, the State Board of Regents requested an outside source be placed on the board of trustees. This was an additional signal that government agencies felt Nelson College needed a change in the executive office. In the end, Bowen announced his retirement during his annual address to Nelson College in 2008. While he remained in office for the rest of the fiscal year, the level of scrutiny severely marginalized his ability to wield the power of the executive office (J. Woodsman, personal communication, November 23, 2009).

Part II: A New President at Nelson College

Aside from the obvious notion that a new leader plays an integral role in the organization, the selection of a president allows the organization to define its needs; the organization then changes from the new perspective he or she brings (Gilmore, 1988). Hence, transitioning leadership, especially on the executive level, plays an important role in the success of the institution.

Thomas North Gilmore (1988, p. 8) writes, "we often dramatically underinvest in these high-leverage opportunities, relying on luck rather than intelligent strategies for success." These strategies differ in each individual scenario, but share common threads that allow a college president to actively prepare for their entry into office. In this process, it is crucial that the new executive remains concerned with obtaining and evaluating information about their new organization, resists the urge to utilize presidential authority too quickly, strategizes how to effectively act on new information and connect with key constituencies (McLaughlin, 1996; Jentz, 1982). The following section will analyze the concepts of strategic entry into the executive office using Nelson College as a case example.

The Interim. As John Bowen stepped down from the podium after announcing his retirement a new phase in the history of the college began. Nelson College, which had never faced a transition in the executive office, was moving into unknown territory. With no institutional memory for this event, the interim process would be filled with fascination and uncertainty.

Indeed, this is a common occurrence during this phase. Organizations facing interim leadership are often disturbed by the heightened sense of uncertainty. As a result, few look to take on long-term projects, fearing that the new leader's vision won't align with the initiative. Speculation begins as to the new direction the institution may take, and in turn, many view any constructive movement as a symbol for the choice of new leadership (Gilmore, 1988).

Angela Long, Nelson College's Director of Institutional Research, maintains that one of the smartest decisions the board made during the interim process was to appoint an interim president. She explains, "He never used [executive] authority. Instead, he ensured the college would continue to operate. Most importantly, he asked a lot of questions" (A. Long, personal communication, November 24, 2009). Jerry Lucas, who had previously served as a community college president, was recommended by the State Board of Regents to hold the temporary post, and in doing so he embarked in a nine-month fact-finding mission. When a new president was finally chosen, the collected information became a powerful tool for objectively understanding the institution (E. Robinson, personal communication, November 23, 2009).

Dr. Robinson began his tenure as president of Nelson College on July 1, 2009, but his work started when he accepted the position two months prior. "Starting then, I was in constant communication with the board chair and the interim president," he said (personal communication, November 23, 2009). As he learned more about the task ahead of him, he started to formulate a strategic plan for how he would handle his first year in office. In this plan, Robinson outlined objectives that would lead to a successful term as president: compiling data, establishing important relationships, managing expectations, and presenting a new vision.

Compiling Data. Robinson, only five months in, feels he is still in the beginning of the data collection phase. "He's always in meetings, reviewing documents, and doesn't talk very much," says Angela Long. "He's engaged in listening and learning" (A. Long, personal communication, November 24, 2009). He has poured though the reports compiled by Dukes, met with nearly every department on campus, and held a variety of gatherings both inside and outside the college. Perhaps most importantly, Robinson created the Office of Institutional Research to perpetually supply him with accurate information (E. Robinson, personal communication, November 23, 2009).

Experts agree that learning about the organization is the most important distinction between a successful and unsuccessful entry into the executive office. Judith McLaughlin, a Harvard University senior lecturer on higher education administration, states that presidents serving in their second executive post have emphasized the importance of this process, making sure that their collection of information was both comprehensive and deliberate (McLaughlin, 1996).

Within this deliberate approach to collecting data, it is crucial to consider the multiplicity of perspectives available and consider how to synthesize overlapping and competing viewpoints. Robinson and Joseph Moore, President of Lesley University, have taken different approaches to the process of creating a singular understanding from various perspectives. Robinson contends that he listens for threads of understanding, seeing how different perspectives overlap to find common ground, similar to a Venn diagram (E. Robinson, personal communication, November 23, 2009). Moore, on the other hand, finds the commonalities enticing but dangerous. In his view, they offer a generic understanding of the situation. He prefers the difference of opinions, hoping to create a culture of "bright and sharp employees" with different ideas to consider in the search for a correct answer (J. Moore, personal communication, December 7, 2009).

Establishing Relationships. Another part of Robinson's plan is to establish a relationship with key constituencies. This initially came easily to the new president, as the college's staff and faculty were eager to meet the new leader (A. Long, personal communication, November 24, 2009). A more difficult task is identifying key allies that can serve as reliable sources of honest feedback on important initiatives. In establishing these connections, Robinson is seeking meaningful and insightful relationships with people in the local community, external agencies, and members of Nelson's faculty and staff (E. Robinson, personal communication, November 23, 2009).

A central connection is Robinson's relationship with the Nelson College Board of Trustees. He still feels the need to make a stronger connection with all the members of the committee. This process will take time because the board is adjusting to the idea of a new president and an "outsider." Importantly, his communication with the board's chair leading up to his arrival helped create a positive relationship. In turn, the chairman is able to supply Robinson with feedback about his work. In contrast, Moore, who has followed lengthy presidencies at both Lesley University and Empire State College, feels that the board is all too quick to agree with a new president. He feels that too often they validate their own selection process by readily agreeing with the new executive chief (J. Moore, personal communication, December 7, 2009). In either scenario, it is vital for the executive to open the lines of communication, providing accurate and thorough information to the board about their decisions and policies. Additionally, the executive needs to collect honest feedback about their work, avoiding the trappings of trustees too quick to find fault or praise.

Establishing a healthy relationship with the college's faculty and administration has proved to be difficult for Robinson. Complicating this effort is the reorganization that often takes place with executive transitions. To create necessary changes, contracts will be allowed to expire, others within the organization will be promoted and interview processes will take place to look at outside candidates (K. Lowe, personal communication, November 24, 2009). Those working their way up the previous management ladder have taken the changes as confounding acts that show little respect to the organization and its culture (Anonymous #2, December 2, 2009). One executive, who chooses to stay anonymous, says, "There isn't a place for me here anymore."

The use of reorganization, as seen in the case of Nelson College, can be disruptive for some within the organization. For this reason, Gilmore (1988) states that reorganization should be used to align the resources of the institution with the new strategy brought by its leader, to promote the importance of new initiatives, to create increased efficiency in lines of communication, and to revitalize the institution.

Lastly, Robinson has made a continued effort to reach out to students, faculty, and the college's external constituencies. In this process, he has welcomed those at the college into his office to discuss pertinent issues. Additionally, he has become involved in community issues and has taken up residency in the local area. This has given him additional insight into the college and community culture and established his credibility (J. Woodsman, personal communication, November 23, 2009). Similarly, Moore gained credibility in his previous presidency by visiting the college's thirty-six remote sites and found it to be incredibly useful during his years as president (J. Moore, personal communication, December 7, 2009).

Managing Expectations. In the shadow of John Bowen, President Robinson must be careful to deal with the expectations that come with transitional leadership. He admits that many people are interested more in action than giving him time to gather information and deliberate. Managing the expectations of his staff has involved a thoughtful persistence to his entry plan. Woodsman mentions one technique Robinson has used to make people understand his commitment: "I've seen him speak to many different groups. He almost always uses the same line 'This is my prologue. Chapter One begins next year'" (J. Woodsman, personal communication, November 23, 2009). "There are those who are frustrated," says Robinson. "I just have to keep telling them it takes time" (E. Robinson, personal communication, November 23, 2009).

In light of Robinson's preference to wait before wielding executive power, experts offer various opinions on this approach. Many, such as McLaughlin, state that new presidents are tempted to take action quickly but should resist the urge. She adds, "the reality is that they do not yet know enough to make informed decisions" (McLaughlin, 1996, p. 11). Conversely, Gilmore (1988) presents the idea that a leader's "honeymoon phase" must be leveraged to affect organizational change. In this paradigm, a college president has a short timeframe to make powerful decisions before opposition parties hinder change. He states that, in time, the leader may be given less room for error and may no longer be seen as an agent of change by becoming responsible for the status quo.

A New Vision. In synthesizing the concepts presented by McLaughlin and Gilmore, a college president is able to wait before using executive power and leverage the "honeymoon phase" by presenting the college with a new management culture. In Robinson's case, he wanted to present, from his first day on the job, the notion that his office and its decisions are driven by data and policies, and practices are transparent in nature. Additionally, Robinson hopes to promote an organizational culture that is comfortable with challenging the status quo, producing innovative ideas, highly accountable for their work and proud to be a part of the institution. Although he knows the organization will need years to fully adopt his style of leadership, he is faithful that "the ship will take on the personality of its captain" (E. Robinson, personal communication, November 23, 2009).

The first of these policies to promote his new vision, which is equipped to collect information and receive critical information, is the "open door" policy in the executive office (J. Woodsman, personal communication, November 23, 2009). Second, Robinson hopes to create an increased call for data-driven information and accountability. To create an additional call for accountability, Robinson is working closely with the board to define new roles for the trustees (E. Robinson, personal communication, November 23, 2009.). Third, Robinson is attempting to change the executive culture from one that lacked clarity in explaining its decisions to a transparent leadership through open and constant communication with Nelson College's employees, whom he addresses weekly in an office memorandum (K. Lowe, personal communication, November 24, 2009).

Conclusion

The exit and entry of executive leadership presents a powerful moment. In the exit of leadership, an institution must reflect on both successes and failures. With a contentious exit, as was the case at Nelson College, the organization needs to understand what precipitated the call for change and how to successfully move forward. This process should guide the college through the interim process and, more crucially, the hiring process. Though the hiring process was not discussed in this work, it is of incredible value for the organization to act with great deliberation. Of equal importance is the entry of new leadership. The entry process should involve a great deal of information and be conducted with thoughtfulness and purpose. During this process, the executive and the institution must exercise patience to ensure the new relationship between the college and the executive has a chance for lasting success.

References

Claussen, N. (September 27, 2006). "Families Who Lost Snowden Land to Eminent Domain Question Development Deal." Athens News, Sept. 27, 2006. Retrieved December 2, 2009, from http://www.athensnews.com/component/content/article/1-local-news/ 7666-families_who_lost_snowden_land_to_eminent_domain
Jentz, B. (1982). ENTRY: The Hiring, Start-Up, and Supervision of Administrators. New York: McGraw Hill.

Kneale, K. "Is Nepotism So Bad?" *Forbes*, June 20, 2009. Forbes.com. Retrieved December 4, 2009.

McLaughlin, J. (1996). *Leadership Transitions: The New College President*. San Francisco: Jossey-Bass.

National Center for Education Statistics, Integrated Postsecondary Education Data System (2002). Retrieved December 3, 2009, from IPEDS Data Center Web site: http://nces.ed.gov/ipeds/datacenter/

MATTHEW WALDMAN *is a 2010 graduate of the Harvard Graduate School of Education.*

INDEX

Abramson, A., 88, 89
Adaptive failure, 79
African Americans, 29–30, 33
African Methodist Church, 32
Ainslie, Carol, 17
Albany State University, 33, 35
Ambrose, S., 61, 63, 65
American Abstract Expressionist movement, 84
American Association of University Professors (AAUP), 71; Committee on College and University Governance, 73; "Joint Statement," 71, 73–74
American Federation of Teachers, 72
American Medical Association, 33
Anderson, L. A., 15
Anglican Church, 95
Appleton, R., 32
Arndt, J. E., 63
Art & Science Group, LLC, 51, 52
"Art at Brandeis" (*New York Times*), 87
Art Institute of Boston (AIB), 52–53
"Assistant Historical Director's Email Announcing the Decision" (SavetheWrenCross.org), 95–96
Atlanta, Georgia, 29
Atlanta City University Center, 33–34
Atlanta University Center, 31
Aurora, New York, 50
Austin, A., 62–65

Babson, Roger, 5
Babson College (Wellesley, Massachusetts): background to Norovirus health crisis at, 5–6; consolidation of crisis response power to deans at, 8–10; Crisis Team, 8, 9; Health Services, 7; lessons from, for other institutions, 12–13; long-term changes at, as result of Norovirus health crisis, 11–12; Management Plan, 8; outbreak of Norovirus health crisis at, 6–8; relationship of, with other community members, 10–11; relationship of, with Wellesley Board of Health, 10; reopening campus at, 11
Baldridge, V. J., 89

Baldwin, R. G., 62, 65, 66, 68
Barber-Scotia College (Concord, North Carolina), 29, 31–33; question of closing, 34–35
Barnard College (New York City), 52
Bataille, G., 62–66
Baylor, R. E., 29
Bernstein, Leonard, 90
Bess, J., 65
"Best Colleges 2010" (*U.S. News and World Report*), 55
"Best of Business" (*New Hampshire Business Review*), 74
Birnbaum, R., 71, 73
Blackburn, R. T., 64, 65
Boice, R., 65
Bok, D., 72
Bolman, L., 77
Bombardieri, M., 50, 51
Bornstein, R., 100
Boston Globe, 87, 88
Bowen, John (pseudonym), 105–109, 112
Brandeis Justice, The, 87
Brandeis University (Waltham, Massachusetts), 83–91; brief organizational history of, 84–86; Ford Hall, 85; soul of, 85
Broskie, C., 98
Brown, B., 62–66
Bruton Parish Church (Williamsburg, Virginia), 95, 98
Bryn Mawr College (Bryn Mawr, Pennsylvania), 52
Bureau of Labor Statistics, 40, 43

Calefati, J., 50
Cambridge, Massachusetts, 52
Carnegie Foundation, 61
Carothers, Robert, 41
Centers for Disease Control, 5–6
Central State University, 32–33, 35
Chin, S., 54–55
"Choosing Strategies for Change" (*Harvard Business Review*), 95
Christians, 96
Clark, S., 61, 62, 65
Clark-Atlanta University, 31, 33–34

Claussen, N., 108
COCE. *See* Southern New Hampshire University (SNHU) College of Online and Continuing Learning (COCE)
Cochrane, A., 97, 98
Cole, Mark, 99
College of William and Mary (Williamsburg, Virginia), 93–101; Christian roots of, 97; Committee on Religion in a Public University, 97, 98; and Gateway William and Mary program, 94–95, 99, 100; and National Collegiate Athletic Association logo crisis, 93–94, 100; Royal Charter of 1693, 96; Sex Worker's Art Show, 98–101; "The Tribe" athletic team and logo, 93–94; Wren Chapel, 95–98; Wren Cross controversy at, 95–101
"College of William and Mary Receives NCAA Ruling on Athletic Logo" (College of William and Mary Office of University Relations), 94
Concord, North Carolina, 29
Connolly, M. R., 94
Corcoran, M., 61, 62, 65
Cota, A., 94, 98
Council of the Princeton University Community, 20
Couturier, L., 39
Crellin, M. A., 71
Cross, Dolores, 30, 34
Cunningham, A., 39
Curtis, P., 63

Dallas, Texas, 29
Deal, T., 66, 77
Dean, C., 72
Dillon, P., 83
Distributive leadership, 80
Doncaster, B., 53
Dow Jones Industrial Average, 18

Eckel, P., 72, 73, 77
Economic crisis, time of: and attention to financial aid, 23; and continuous unfolding of management actions in response to, 24–25; conveying meaning of, 15–25; deteriorating outlooks and escalating, 18–21; and economic collapse of 2008, 15, 18; and endowment-related statistics, 2008–2009, 16; and setting tone and assessing damage for period of October 2008-January 2009, 18–21; and trust in prudent planning, 23–24

Edgers, G., 88
"Editorial: Nichol Botched Handling of Cross" *(Flat Hat),* 96
Ehrenberg, R. G., 62
Eisgruber, Christopher, 17, 20
Emery, T., 3
Empire State College, 111
"Endowment Distribution to be Reduced by 8 Percent" *(Harvard Magazine),* 22
Esposito, G., 39
Etchemendy, John, 17, 21, 24

Fain, P., 39
Fairweather, J., 64
Farrell, D., 61
"FAS Dean Details $220-Million Budget" *(Harvard Magazine),* 22
Faust, Drew Gilpin (Harvard University), 17, 19–22, 24
Fellman, G., 84
Finkelstein, M., 61, 63–65
Fisher, M., 94
Fisk University, 32–33, 35
"Floating signifier," 71–72
Florida Memorial University, 32, 35
"Former Morris Brown College President, Financial Aid Director Indicted for Fraud" *(Diverse: Black Issues in Higher Education),* 30
Forst, Edward, 17, 20
Francis, Norman, 36
Franklin W. Olin College of Engineering, 11
Freeland, R. M., 84, 85
Freeland, Richard, 44
French, Barbara (pseudonym), 107
French, Peter, 87
Frost, Richard, 7
Fryer, R., 33

Gappa, J., 62–65
Gasman, M., 29–31
Gateway William and Mary program (College of William and Mary), 94–95
Gatlin, G., 53
"Gene Nichol's Email Confirming Order to Remove Cross from Wren Chapel" (SavetheWrenCross.org), 96
Georgetown University (Washington, D.C.), 6
Georgia State University, 31
Gerber, Larry, 73
Geroux, B., 100
Gilmore, Thomas North, 109, 110, 112
Goal ambiguity, 89

Godson, S., 95
Goldstein, S., 5
Goodman, Michael, 45, 46
Grambling University, 32–33, 35
Grassley, Charles, 25
Greenstone, M., 33
Groover, J., 32
Guillen, A., 98

H1N1 virus, coordinating appropriate crisis response to, 5
Haley, V., 96, 97
Hanno, Dennis, 6, 7, 9–10, 12, 13
Hardy, M., 97
Harp, Seth, 32
Harvard Magazine, 22
Harvard University (Cambridge, Massachusetts), 15, 18–21, 43, 110; budgetary outlook for, during period of February to April 2009, 21–22; capital planning during fiscal crisis at, 22–23; deteriorating outlooks and escalating responses (February-April 2009) at, 21–23; endowment-related statistics of 2008–2009 from, 16; investing during fiscal crisis at, 22; reaction to economic crisis at, 19–20; setting tone and assessing damage (October 2008-January 2009) at, 18–21; staffing during fiscal crisis at, 22; timeline of public messaging on economic crises, 2008–2009, 17
Hatch, K., 11
Hawkins, D., 32–33, 36
HBCUs. *See* Historically Black colleges and universities (HBCUs)
Heifitz, R., 79
Hennessy, John (Stanford University), 17, 19–21, 23–25
Herrmann, M., 32
Higgins, M. (pseudonym), 106
Historically Black colleges and universities (HBCUs), loss of accreditation at, 29–37; and Albany State University, 32; and Barber-Scotia College, 31–32, 34–35; and Central State University, 32; and Fisk University, 32–33; and Florida Memorial University, 32; and Grambling State University, 32–33; and Morris Brown College, 29–31, 33–34; and Paul Quinn College, 32; possible corrective actions during fiscal crisis for, 35–37; and relevance of HBCUs to higher education, 33; and Savannah State University, 32;

and Texas College, 32–33; and Tougaloo College, 32; and Wilberforce University, 32–33
Hogan, Andrew, 86
Holub, Robert, 43–46
Hope College (Holland, Michigan), 6, 7
"Hope College Estimates 400 Students, Staff Struck by Norovirus-like Illness" (*Grand Rapids Press*), 6
Huston, T., 61, 63, 65

Institutional culture, contested, 93–101
Internal Revenue Services (IRS), 25
International students of color, 29
Israel-Palestine debates, 90

Jakubson, G. H., 62
Jan, T., 42, 50, 51, 88, 90
Jaschik, S., 32, 51
Jentz, B., 109
Jewish community, 85, 90
Jewish cultural traditions, 89
Jewish faith, 84
Jewish identity, 85, 89
Jewish influence on American society, 90
Jewish philanthropic community, 86
Johnsrud, L. K., 61–65
Jordan, J., 39, 40
Journal of Higher Education, 94
Joyner, Tom, 31, 34

Kaine, Timothy, 99
Kaplan, R. S., 15
Kelderman, E., 31, 32, 34
Kennedy, R., 87
Kezar, A., 71–73, 77
Kinzie, J., 49–50
Kinzie, S., 6
Kirsch, H., 88
Kocar, Debra, 54–56
Kosher crisis of 1987, 89
Kotter, J. P., 95
Kramer, R., 78–80
Kratzok, S., 49
Krauss, Marty, 87, 88

Lawrence, J., 64
Leading a Small College or University: A Convention That Never Ends (Peterson), 96
LeBlanc, P., 74–76
Lechuga, V. M., 71
Legitimacy in the Academic Presidency (Bornstein), 100

Lehman's, collapse at, 15, 17
Lesley, Edith, 52
Lesley College (Cambridge, Massachusetts), 52–57; lessons learned from, 56
Lesley University, 111
Lesley University Archives, 52
Lewis, D., 61, 62, 65
Long, Angela (pseudonym), 110, 111
Lowe, K. (pseudonym), 106–108, 111, 113
Lucas, Jerry (pseudonym), 110
Lynott, Patricia, 75

Madoff, Bernie, 86
Mahoney, B., 93, 95
Mallon, W. T., 74
Marder, R., 86
Marks, C. M., 5
Massachusetts, 39–47; community colleges, 73; declining state support for public universities in, 42–45
Massachusetts Budget, 2009, 42
Massachusetts Department of Public Health, 7, 8
Maurano, Steve, 40–42, 46
McGlothlin, James, 97
McKenna, Margaret, 53
McLaughlin, J. B., 73, 85, 109, 110, 112
Mendillo, J. L., 15
Meola, O., 99
Michigan, 39
Middle East, 86
Miller-Bernal, L., 49–52, 56
Mills College (Oakland, California), 51, 57
Minor, J. T., 77
Moody's Investor Service, 18–20, 25, 89
Moore, Joseph, 111, 112
Moore, M. T., 50
Morehouse College, 34
Morgan, T., 55
Morin, S. A., 93
Morris Brown College (Atlanta, Georgia), 29–32; question of closing, 33–34
"Morris Brown President Sentenced" (Diverse Black Issues in Higher Education), 30
Mortenson, Tom, 46, 47
Mount Holyoke College (South Hadley, Massachusetts), 52; Office of Communications, 52

National Association of College and University Business Officers, 16, 18
National Center for Educational Statistics, 51; Integrated Postsecondary Education Data System, 107

National Center for Public Policy in Higher Education, 40
National Collegiate Athletic Association (NCAA), 93, 94
National Survey of Student Engagement (NSSE), 49
Native American imagery, 93–94
Native American peoples, 93–94
NCAA. See National Collegiate Athletic Association (NCAA)
Needham, Massachusetts, 10
Nelson College (pseudonym): and Barbara French, 107; data compiling at, 110–111; divisions in workplace at, 107; end of Nelson presidency at, 108–109; establishing relationships at, 111–112; executive transition at, 109–110; external conflict at, 107; and Lake Gunderson, 107–108; leadership culture at, 105–107; legal battles at, 108; managing expectations at, 112; new president at, 109–113; new vision for, 112–113; rapid change and legitimacy at, 105–113; unraveling presidency at, 105–109
Neubauer, M., 86, 89
New England Board of Higher Education, 45
New Hampshire Business Review, 74
New Jersey, 39
"New Logo a Disappointment" (Flat Hat), 94
New York Times, 85, 87, 88
Newman, Betsy, 6–13
Nicas, J., 44
Nichol, G. R., 93–101; State of the College address, 97
"Nichol Discusses Wren Cross Decision with BOV" (savethewrencross.org), 96
Noonan, E., 50
Norman, M., 61, 63, 65
Norovirus, 5–13; definition of, 5–6; outbreak of, at Georgetown University (Washington, D.C.), 6; outbreak of, at Hope College (Holland, Michigan), 6
North Hampton, Massachusetts, 52
NSSE. See National Survey of Student Engagement (NSSE)

Oakland, California, 51
Obama administration, 43
Olson, G., 71–72
Orwell, George, 72

Palestine, 86
Palestinian Art incident of 2006, 89

Paul Quinn College (Dallas, Texas), 29, 32; question of closing, 34–35

Pell Grants, 40, 43, 46

Pell Institute for the Study of Opportunity in Higher Education, 46

Peterson, H. L., 96

Petkofsky, A., 93, 97, 99

Pinkerton, J., 96, 97

Pittinsky, T. L., 77, 78

Postsecondary Education Opportunity State Reports, 39–41, 43, 44

Potts, Sammie, 32

Poulson, S. L., 51–52, 56

Powell, Michael, 98, 99

Powell, T., 31

Powers, E., 51

Princeton Alumni Weekly, 20

Princeton University (Princeton, New Jersey), 15–25; capital planning during fiscal crisis at, 22–23; and Council of the Princeton University Community, 20; deteriorating outlooks and escalating responses during period of February-April 2009 at, 21–23; endowment-related statistics of 2008-2009 from, 16; investing during financial crisis at, 22; setting tone and assessing damage (October 2008-January 2009) at, 18–21; staffing during fiscal crisis at, 22; and striking different tone in responding to economic crisis, 20–21; timeline of public messaging on economic crises, 2008–2009, 17

Pritchett, Stanley J., Sr., 31

Rahman, N., 88

Reck, R., 85

Regis College (Weston, Massachusetts), 50, 51, 57; Admissions Office, 51

Reid, A., 63

Reinharz, Jehuda, 85–88, 90

Rhode Island, 39–45; declining state support for public universities in, 39–42; State Higher Education Finance Report, 39

Rhode Island State Budget Executive Summary, 40

Richmond, Virginia, 99–100

Rizzo, M. R., 62

Robinson, E. (pseudonym), 106, 110–113

Rose Art Museum: Board of Directors, 87; Board of Overseers, 88; Board of Trustees, 88–90; and Brandeis University, 84–86; crisis at, 83–91; and Future of Rose Committee, 88; organizational

tendencies of, 89–90; outcomes of crisis at, 88–89; setting stage for crisis at, 86–88

Rosser, V. J., 61–65

Rousseau, D. M., 62

Rush, M., 84, 87

Russell, B. C., 61

Russell, J., 53

Ryerson, L. M., 50

Sachar, Abram, 84, 89, 90

SACS. *See* Southern Association of Colleges and Schools (SACS)

Sander, L., 30–31

SAT scores, 55

Savannah State University, 33, 35

SaveTheWrenCross.org, 97, 98

Schexnider, A., 33

Schlesinger, Leonard A. (President of Babson College), 7–11, 13, 95

Schragle-Law, S., 74–76

Schworm, P., 42, 85, 86, 88

Senior faculty careers: and administration leadership, 61–62; autonomy and pursuit of knowledge in, 64–65; recommendations for, 66–68; resources and support for, 62–63; stress in, 61–68; and workload issue, 65–66

Seven Sisters colleges, 52

Seymour, A., Jr., 31

Shared governance, 3; and changing realities that re-prioritize governance, 72–73; criticisms to the calls for revision and examining tenability of, 73–74; culture, symbolism, and analysis of, in changing times, 76–77; examples of, in global age, 74–76; future of, 71–80; intergroup relationship and navigating change in, 77–80; internal and external stresses on, 71–72; re-endowing, while preserving collegiality, 80

Sheldon, M., 51

Shuster, J., 61, 63–65

Simmonson, Marcia Testa, 10

Singh, Parvesh, 30

Skillen, L., 54–55

Sodexo, Inc., 11

Sorrell, Michael, 35

South Hadley, Massachusetts, 52

Southern Association of Colleges and Schools (SACS), 30–33, 35, 36

Southern New England, 39, 47

Southern New Hampshire University (SNHU) College of Online and Continuing

Learning (COCE), 74–77; analysis of governance structure at, 76
S&P 500 Index, 15
Spelman College, 34
Stanford University (Stanford, California), 15–25; budgeting during fiscal crisis at, 21–22; capital planning during fiscal crisis at, 22–23; deteriorating outlooks and escalating responses during period of February-April 2009 at, 21–23; endowment-related statistics of 2008-2009 from, 16; investing during fiscal crisis at, 22; reaction to economic crisis at, 19–20; setting tone and assessing damage (October 2008-January 2009) at, 18–21; staffing during fiscal crisis at, 22; timeline of public messaging on economic crises, 2008–2009, 17
State Higher Education Executive Officers: Finance Report, 39, 43; State Facts, 43
State support, declining: and Massachusetts, 42–45; possible solutions for and analysis of, 45–47; and Rhode Island, 39–42
Stevens, R., 20
Strauss, David, 51, 52, 57
Strauss, N. C., 25
Streit, C., 52–56
Stritter, F. T., 63
Sullivan, Timothy J., 93
Sunkin, A., 50

Tammaro, Susan, 51
Tarantino, M., 52
Texas, 32
Texas College (Tyler, Texas), 35
Thomas, Michael, 45, 46
Tierney, W. G., 71, 77
Tilghman, Shirley M. (Princeton University), 17, 20, 21, 23, 24
Title IX, 50–51
Todor, A., 99
Tougaloo College, 32, 35
Trice, A., 62–65
Trust Universe Comparison Service, 15
Turner, J. L., 65

UMass-Amherst. See University of Massachusetts, Amherst
University of Massachusetts, Amherst, 42–44; College of Natural Science and Mathematics and the Environment, 44
University of Massachusetts, Dartmouth, 45

University of Massachusetts Fact Sheets (Office of Institutional Research), 44
University of Massachusetts system, 44
University of Rhode Island, 41; Office of Institutional Research, 42
U.S. Department of Education, 30–32, 61
U.S. News and World Report, 55, 85
U.S. Senate Committee on Finance, 23

Venerable, Grant, 30
Virginia, 42, 97; General Assembly, 97; House of Delegates, 99–100
Virginia Gazette, 98
Vogel, C., 87

"Wake up the World" campaign (Lesley College), 53
Wald, M., 85
Waldman, M., 105
Walker, B., 94
Waltham, Massachusetts, 83
Warner, Jack, 41, 44, 47
Washington, D.C., 6
Wasserman, A., 11
Weick, K., 77
Wellesley, Massachusetts, 5, 10; Board of Health, 6–8, 10; Health Department, 10
Wellesley College (Wellesley, Massachusetts), 51–52, 57; "Commission on the Future of the College," 52
Wells College (Aurora, New York), 50, 51, 57; External Relations Office, 50
Western Interstate Commission for Higher Education, 45
Weston, Massachusetts, 50
"What's In a Name" (Journal of Higher Education), 94
Wilberforce University, 32–33
Williamsburg, Virginia, 93
Williamsburg colony, 94
"W&M Takes Comments on Nichol's Performance" (Richmond Times Dispatch), 99
Women's College Coalition, 49
Women's colleges: future of, 56–57; and Lesley College, 52–56; long tradition of, 49–50; push for coeducation in, 50–52; tough questions facing, 49–57
Woods, S. E., 63
Woodsman, J. (pseudonym), 105, 108, 109, 112, 113
World War II, 47

Wren Cross controversy (College of William and Mary), 95–98
Wright, A., 97, 98, 100

Xavier University, 33, 36

Yale University, 25
Yardley, Sharon, 6–8

Zak, E., 10

ORDER FORM SUBSCRIPTION AND SINGLE ISSUES

DISCOUNTED BACK ISSUES:

Use this form to receive 20% off all back issues of *New Directions for Higher Education*.
All single issues priced at **$23.20** (normally $29.00)

TITLE	ISSUE NO.	ISBN

Call 888-378-2537 or see mailing instructions below. When calling, mention the promotional code JBNND to receive your discount. For a complete list of issues, please visit www.josseybass.com/go/ndhe

SUBSCRIPTIONS: (1 YEAR, 4 ISSUES)

☐ New Order   ☐ Renewal

U.S.	☐ Individual: $89	☐ Institutional: $259
CANADA/MEXICO	☐ Individual: $89	☐ Institutional: $299
ALL OTHERS	☐ Individual: $113	☐ Institutional: $333

Call 888-378-2537 or see mailing and pricing instructions below.
Online subscriptions are available at www.onlinelibrary.wiley.com

ORDER TOTALS:

Issue / Subscription Amount: $ _____

Shipping Amount: $ _____
(for single issues only – subscription prices include shipping)

Total Amount: $ _____

SHIPPING CHARGES:
First Item $5.00
Each Add'l Item $3.00

(No sales tax for U.S. subscriptions. Canadian residents, add GST for subscription orders. Individual rate subscriptions must be paid by personal check or credit card. Individual rate subscriptions may not be resold as library copies.)

BILLING & SHIPPING INFORMATION:

☐ **PAYMENT ENCLOSED:** *(U.S. check or money order only. All payments must be in U.S. dollars.)*

☐ **CREDIT CARD:**   ☐ VISA   ☐ MC   ☐ AMEX

Card number _____ Exp. Date _____

Card Holder Name_____ Card Issue # _____

Signature _____ Day Phone _____

☐ **BILL ME:** *(U.S. institutional orders only. Purchase order required.)*

Purchase order # _____
Federal Tax ID 13559302 • GST 89102-8052

Name _____

Address_____

Phone_____ E-mail_____

Copy or detach page and send to: **John Wiley & Sons, PTSC, 5th Floor**
989 Market Street, San Francisco, CA 94103-1741

Order Form can also be faxed to: **888-481-2665**

PROMO JBNND